DATE			

MARCEL BÉNABOU

Dump This Book While

Jette ce livre avant qu'il soit trop tard

You Still Can!

Translated by Steven Rendall
with an introduction by Warren Motte

•

UNIVERSITY OF NEBRASKA PRESS

LINCOLN AND LONDON

Publication of this volume was assisted by
The Virginia Faulkner Fund, established in memory of
Virginia Faulkner, editor-in-chief of the University
of Nebraska Press

Library of Congress Cataloging in Publication Data
Bénabou, Marcel.
[Jette ce livre avant qu'il soit trop tard. English]
Dump this book while you still can! /
Marcel Bénabou; translated by Steven Rendall; with
an introduction by Warren Motte.
p. cm. (Stages: v. 18)
ISBN 0-8032-1319-0 (cloth: alk. paper) –
ISBN 0-8032-6186-1 (paperback: alk. paper)
I. Rendall, Steven
II. Title. III. Series: Stages (Series): v. 18.
PQ2662.E4714J4813 2001
848'.91407—dc21   2001017104

CONTENTS

Introduction Caveat Lector

WARREN MOTTE

Dump This Book While You Still Can! Gentle Reader, you
have just been bludgeoned by one of the most bizarre titles
you have ever encountered, and it is little wonder if you are
reeling under its impact. It will provide some small consolation
to learn that the hero of this novel, a reader very much like
yourself, finds himself faced with a book with an identical title;
and his initial reactions may very well resemble your own. He
doesn't like to be addressed directly in book titles; he wonders if
he is the object of a farce; he feels that he is being treated with
arrogance and off-handedness. Yet he recognizes, as we do, that
writers use titles in order to pique their readers' curiosity in
various ways. A title can, for example, suggest that the book it
designates contains a marvelous vastness of information, spec-
ulation, and insight. The Russians are masters of that form, with
dizzying coordinations such as Tolstoy's *War and Peace*, Dos-
toevsky's *Crime and Punishment*, and Vasily Grossman's *Life
and Fate*. Some titles are deliberately enigmatic, like Melville's
Moby-Dick and Harry Mathews's *Tlooth*. Some are provocative
in other ways; one thinks of Robert Coover's *Spanking the Maid*,
and Madonna surely deserves an honorable mention for *Sex*. If
any title creates a certain degree of suspense, some titles wager
on that function more heavily than others, for instance, Henry
James's *What Maisie Knew*, Georges Perec's *What Little Bicycle
with Chrome Handlebars at the Far End of the Courtyard?*, and
Italo Calvino's *If on a Winter's Night a Traveler*. Other titles, like
Mark Harris's *Wake Up, Stupid* and Abbie Hoffman's *Steal This
Book!*, seem to leap off the cover at us in a naked exhortation
calculated to disturb the peace of mind that we both expect and

deserve when we open a new book. That, of course, is the category to which *this* title belongs, though it may seem to be a particularly perverse – and apparently self-defeating – example of the species.

So who is the man responsible for it? Marcel Bénabou was born into a Sephardic family in Meknès, Morocco in 1939. He went to study at the Lycée Louis-le-Grand in Paris when he was seventeen years old, and from there matriculated at the École Normale Supérieure, that elite institution of higher learning that has put its stamp on a good portion of the French intelligentsia. Bénabou earned his doctorate and has for many years been a professor at the Université de Paris VII, where he teaches Roman history; his major contribution to that field is a learned volume entitled *La résistance africaine à la romanisation* [1976; The African resistance to romanization]. Deeply and indeed, by his own admission, obsessively interested in literature since his early childhood years, Marcel Bénabou collaborated on a series of writerly projects in the 1960s with his friend Georges Perec. Like Perec, Bénabou became a member of the Ouvroir de Littérature Potentielle [Workshop of Potential Literature], or 'Oulipo,' a group of writers and mathematicians founded in 1960 by Raymond Queneau and François Le Lionnais, devoted to the study of literary forms both old and new. Bénabou has served the Oulipo long and nobly as the group's 'Definitively Provisional Secretary.' In 1986, Bénabou published his first book-length work of literature, whose title, *Pourquoi je n'ai écrit aucun de mes livres* [*Why I Have Not Written Any of My Books*], is perhaps just as disconcerting as the present one; it appeared in an English translation by David Kornacker at the University of Nebraska Press in 1996. *Dump This Book While You Still Can!* followed, published in France in 1992. *Jacob, Ménahem et Mimoun: Une Épopée familiale* [*Jacob, Menahem, and Mimoun: A*

Family Epic] is his latest book; it appeared in France in 1995, and was translated for Nebraska by Steven Rendall in 1998. Reflecting upon Marcel Bénabou's career as a writer, one is struck by a curious phenomenon: with only three books in his oeuvre, he has established a firm place for himself in the contemporary avant-garde. I say 'oeuvre' advisedly, because it is a highly calculated, very organic body of work, conceived as a strongly articulative whole, animated by a fresh literary imagination and an exceptionally subtle mind, leavened by the ironic, self-deprecating humor that has become Bénabou's trademark.

Dump This Book is less confessional and more overtly novelistic than Bénabou's two other books, between which it nestles. To anyone familiar with those works, however, its style will be immediately recognizable, for it is marked by the same kinds of complexities, convolutions, and recursiveness. The syntax of this novel is just as tortured as the narrator's mind seems to be, and it should be noted here that Steven Rendall has done a superb job – once again – in rendering this difficult Bénabaldian prose into English, following its daunting meanders unhesitatingly, step by step. Like Bénabou's other books, too, the form of *Dump This Book* is highly organized; this is most obvious in the 'symphonic' structure that he has proposed here, and within which a variety of themes and effects find harmony. Finally, just like *Why I Have Not Written Any of My Books* and *Jacob, Menahem, and Mimoun*, *Dump This Book* is founded upon a game. That consideration becomes apparent in the very first pages of the novel, where a man, the narrator, is reading a book whose very first lines warn him to throw the book away; and he is finding it very difficult going. Sound familiar?

Clearly, Bénabou is playing with us here. I do not mean to suggest, however, that he is being frivolous; on the contrary, the game he proposes is animated by an intense seriousness of purpose. One recalls that Goethe characterized his *Faust* as 'this very serious jest,' and that Thomas Mann borrowed the same term to describe *The Magic Mountain*. In a similar vein, Bénabou invites us to engage in an articulative, playful exchange whose principal figures are author, narrator, and reader, and through which the meaning of this text will be produced. Our role has been scripted for us, yet we are free to interpret that role in the way we see fit. The narrator does not enjoy quite the same degree of freedom. He is benighted, poor soul, by the book he tries to read; and toward the end of the novel he will confess his own defeat. At that point, the specific kind of game that Bénabou is playing becomes clear. It might be called 'loser wins,' and (as Michel Beaujour has pointed out) it is a game that is particularly dear to the avant-garde. One can of course play a game according to traditional rules; but that possibility does not interest Bénabou, for he finds those rules impossible to follow, and in any case, they have given rise to an imposing corpus of texts that he cannot pretend to rival. One can, however, turn one's back on the rules – or pretend to do so – and declare oneself out of the game, a move that offers a set of quite different possibilities. In effect, what this entails is a reconfiguration of the game according to new protocols, ones which, upon examination, depend closely and symmetrically upon the old ones. For the eschewal of conventional rhetoric is itself a rhetorical gesture; and when Bénabou's narrator declares himself defeated, we must take his words in a rhetorical manner. By analogy, Bénabou intends that we should read *through* his narrator's lamentations. When the narrator castigates, for instance, the injunctions, the interjections, the interrogations that he sees on the page of the book he's trying to read, we are prompted to reflect upon the page of the book that *we* are reading, and upon the ironical, duplicitous, and playful relations that yoke those two pages. When toward the end of the novel the narrator says that his project is hovering on the brink of failure, we are encouraged to reflect on Bénabou's own project, one that is likewise drawing to an end, but which may just eventuate in something other than outright failure.

Our role – should we accept to play it – demands the same kind of brazen ruse, the sort of cheerful bad faith, that Bénabou displays throughout his work, as he turns the categories of possibility and impossibility, success and failure, on their heads and exploits them to his advantage. We must play what is said against what is meant, what we're told against what is whispered in our ear, and what we read against what we understand.

Thematically, Marcel Bénabou's other books focus on the activity of writing. *Dump This Book*, however, is a novel about reading, about its delights and its discontents. As we read over the narrator's shoulder, his reading ironically mirrors our own, and we are constantly confronted with our own reading act, with the habitual gestures, strategies, and inferences that we deploy when we read. If the narrator's struggles are at least modestly heroic, so too are ours; and in that Bénabou positions us as protagonists in the drama he constructs. He suggests moreover that there are a variety of affinities and mutual complementarities that prevail between reading and writing; that the author's efforts to create meaning are closely reciprocal of the reader's; and that the fundamental economy of literature is not one of mere production and reception, but rather one that is far more articulative and participatory. In short, he has furnished a generous space for his reader in this novel; and he will ask his reader to inhabit that space in creative ways.

The volume that the narrator of this novel is holding in his hands is full of admonishment and advice, just like the volume we are holding. Yet most of the time, he is not particularly reassured by those apostrophes. He worries about becoming lost in the book – all the more so when the author confesses that he, too, is lost. Each time the narrator picks up the book, the text seems to have changed. He finds it more and more difficult to read and frets that he has set out upon a journey that will eventually leave him utterly illiterate. His readerly struggles even pervade his dreams: he has a nightmare in which the letters on the page before him melt into a sort of magma and refuse all of his efforts to organize them in meaningful ways. He wonders if he hasn't exhausted himself as a reader, like a man who, after a night of love, longs merely for a glass of water. Two activities are at issue as the narrator grapples with his book: reading, very simply conceived, and interpretation. The narrator finds the former thorny enough, and he rehearses a variety of strategies in order simply to *read*. He focuses upon individual words, hoping to find hidden meanings therein; he examines the letters themselves, wondering if they would signify better in different combinations; he reads the text aloud, hoping thereby to understand it. The narrator's problems with simple reading being what they are, it is less than surprising to find that his interpretational efforts are also foredoomed. He reflects on the great medieval tradition of exegesis and upon the distinguished commentators and glossarists who animated it, how they could read *through* the various arcana – rebuses, anagrams, chronograms, cryptograms – of the texts they dealt with. But he, of course, is not one of them. He will try a variety of heuristics on for size, discarding them one after the other as each proves to be of no avail.

Even as this book defeats him, he remains convinced that it signifies mightily and suspects that it may in fact represent something like the book-of-all-books, a construct dear to the Cabalists and to Mallarmé alike. And to Marcel Bénabou, too, it must be noted, for Bénabou's books constantly and inevitably point their readers to the literary tradition that precedes them and in which they aspire to take root. In *Dump This Book*, for instance, one finds a truly astonishing number of references to other writers. I note them here in order to provide some idea of the dimensions of his allusive practice (and also, I admit, for the simple joy of enumeration): Aesop, Pythagoras, Sophocles, Socrates, Plato, Aristotle, Demosthenes, Cicero, Virgil, Seneca, Martial, Dante, Abraham Abulafia, Rabelais, Bonaventure des Périers, Scève, Montaigne, Francis Bacon, Shakespeare, François Maynard, Hobbes, La Rochefoucauld, La Fontaine, Boileau, La Bruyère, Montesquieu, Lessing, Georg Christoph Lichtenberg, Louis-Sébastien Mercier, Goethe, Walter Scott, Schopenhauer, Balzac, Hugo, Gogol, Poe, Baudelaire, Flaubert, Lautréamont, Huysmans, Rimbaud, Jules Laforgue, Mallarmé, Verlaine, Proust, Valéry, Jarry, Apollinaire, Kafka, Maurice Sachs, Pierre Reverdy, Jorge Luis Borges, Henri Michaux, Raymond Queneau, Maurice Blanchot, René Char, Malcolm Lowry, Italo Calvino, and Georges Perec.

It should be remarked, however, that the intertextual play in Bénabou's writing ranges far beyond mere reference and mocks the notion of literary allusion as we commonly understand it. The insistent references to other writers serve undoubtedly to put Bénabou's erudition as a reader of literature on display; they locate his own books in a context of literary tradition; and they suggest the kinds of directions that he intends to pursue. But their principal function rejoins a far more trenchant and ironically focused metaliterary discourse: these are the writers that beggar Bénabou's *own* writing. Imitation may be the sincerest form of compliment, yet serious literature cares not a whit for compliment. For the paradoxical constraint that serious literature imposes on a writer is to carve something entirely new and original out of a venerable linguistic and cultural patrimony.

That's clearly a tall – and perhaps impossible – order. Yet Marcel Bénabou's books are uncompromisingly grounded in the very notion of the impossible. *Dump This Book* is no exception. Its narrator knows that the shining, immanent perfection he seeks to find when he reads inheres neither in the books he has already read nor in the books he intends to read in the future. He wonders if it might be found in books that he cannot yet even imagine and upon which he will undoubtedly never lay his eyes. For that's the real problem with impossible ideals: their site, in our fevered imagination, is always located around some impossibly distant corner, a place that constantly and maddeningly recedes before us, even as we haltingly approach it. As the narrator casts about in every direction among theories of the book in order to find something that might correspond to his own exalted conception of that ideal, he gradually becomes aware that the ideal book he longs for so desperately is one that, by its very nature, can never be made manifest in mortal form. That lesson is an important one for him, for us, and especially for Marcel Bénabou. How can Bénabou hope to overcome (or at least attenuate) the obstacles in the impossible project to which he has mortgaged body and soul? The short answer is that Bénabou has chosen to write impossible books, fully recognizing – and indeed savoring – the absurdity of that aspiration, turning the very impossibility of his task into his subject. Writing each of his books, he speaks primarily about how the book *might* have been written, granted a set of optimal – and impossible – conditions. What results from that process are books that propose themselves to us principally as virtualities, the vehicles of a literary discourse whose only valid modes are conditional, hypothetical, and interrogative.

Recognizing their impossible character, Marcel Bénabou nonetheless asks us to read his books. He longs for a perfect reader, one who would be equal to the kind of book he would most certainly write, if only he were able. There's the rub, of course: what he's *got*, in point of fact, is not the ideal reader, but rather you and me, with all of our myriad flaws. Perhaps Bénabou would settle for someone who, reading through the imperfections of the books he has written, would envision, shimmering on a distant horizon, the outlines of a perfect book. That's undoubtedly a great deal to ask, yet such terms seem implicit in the contract that Bénabou tenders us here. Its clauses are perhaps less stern, less baldly forward than they may appear on first inspection, for Bénabou asks us for no less than he demands of himself, proposing that we struggle, sweat, and occasionally despair right alongside him as, together, we ponder the very idea of the book. Travails are much easier to bear when they are shared, after all. Moreover, Bénabou carefully lubricates each hinge of this articulative relationship with high good humor: as we watch him write, as he watches us read, as he frets over his writing and we over our reading, some of the more staggering demands that books impose on their writers and their readers become comically apparent. It is precisely in that perspective that *this* book has a great deal to say. Layering ironies upon ironies, alternately haranguing, cajoling, daring, enticing, and encouraging his reader, Marcel Bénabou invites us to think about the ways writers and readers cleave to literature, even when – perhaps particularly when – literature seems to be at its most embattled as a vital cultural form.

A Note on the Translation
STEVEN RENDALL

Because this book is to a large extent generated by the interpretive permutations to which the narrator subjects the text he is trying to read, it raises special problems for the translator. For instance, the French word *pose* (lay down), which appears in the opening sentence, is read backward, producing *Ésope* (Aesop), while *jette* (throw away), which appears in the title of the book as well as in the first sentence, is read homonymically as *je tais* (I leave unsaid). The only way to render this kind of wordplay in another language is to reinvent it in another form, and that is what I have tried to do here. Thus in the corresponding passage on p. 51, I have rung variations on 'dump' and 'throw' (*jette* and *pose*), playing on the relations between 'dump' and 'dumb,' and between 'throw' and 'worth,' in a way that has no literal equivalent in the French text.

Much the same is true of many other passages, though most involved less extensive rewriting. I have also made certain adjustments to make the book more intelligible to a non-French audience. For instance, the character named 'Simon' is the French text appears here as 'Sigmund' in order to make the allusion to Freud clearer, and I have occasionally substituted a reference to an English author or phrase for a French one likely to be unfamiliar to an English-speaking reader.

However, despite my best efforts, and despite Marcel Bénabou's generous advice (for which I heartily thank him!), I have, of course, been unable to render all the allusions and plays on words with which the French text fairly sparkles. I can only hope that my translation conveys a sense of the author's ingenious and often hilarious linguistic inventiveness.

Dump This Book While You Still Can!

There is hardly any merchandise in the world stranger than books: printed by people who don't understand them, sold by people who don't understand them, bound, censored, and read by people who don't understand them, and – better yet – written by people who don't understand them.

– Lichtenberg

OVERTURE

Come on, dump this book. Or better yet, throw it as far away as you can. Right now. Before it's too late. That resolution is your only escape, believe me.

Now look up. Let your weary eyes rest upon the peace of infinite horizons, large spaces punctuated only by trees, rocks, and clouds. Look away from these perverse lines.

What do you expect from them? What can you expect?

If you think you're going to meet a bosom buddy, a new friend with whom you can have one of those intimate conversations you've been dreaming about for such a long time, forget it. Go find someone else to listen to you and console you.

Or maybe you hope that by some miracle you're going to see your own image reflected here, more or less, or that you're suddenly going to recognize a little bit of your own thought. Maybe you even imagine (who knows how far your naïveté will go?) that you're going to find a guaranteed way of recovering the use of your own voice.

Or then again, at the last minute, you've convinced yourself (for you have gradually acquired a taste for certainties!) that things won't begin until you arrive, that you are the indispensable witness without whom nothing that happens here will have any meaning. And you expect to receive your reward for the gift you are going to make.

Unless your only concern is to dispel a moment of boredom, and your only goal is to go as far as you can into foreign territory, to discover worlds you've never seen before, to experience the pleasures and pains you've never had the courage to give to those around you.

Who cares what you expect, anyway? Whatever it is, you're going to be disappointed.

You have nothing in common, believe me, with the shades that are about to dance before your eyes. Their fate was sealed long ago, whereas you are still wondering what you're going to do at the next moment.

So why continue?

Well, you asked for it.

This book, which you have just entered rashly and without precautions, you still don't know that, like me, you're running the risk of getting lost in it.

The text stopped there. The last lines formed a sort of small, compact block occupying only the top part of the page – about a third of it, hardly more, and perhaps a little less. The rest of the page was blank, a fact emphasized by the grayish color of the paper and the poor quality of the material from which it was made.

FIRST MOVEMENT

*Enough effrontery to imitate the charlatans
who display, to attract the curiosity of a crowd at a fair,
a crocodile painted on a bit of canvas, behind which
you find, after you've paid, only a lizard.*
– Victor Hugo

I have to admit that this injunction disconcerted me.

To tell the truth, reader, I don't really like to be addressed directly at the beginning of a book. After all, why should I be interested in recommendations made by some unknown person, not to mention his private thoughts? On the contrary, what I like at the crucial moment of beginning, which is so full of solemnity that it ought finally to be recognized as having the sacred character that ancient religions, in their wisdom, granted it (and which is, moreover, so laden with promises that to do things right one should just begin again, over and over), is that I be treated with the proper discretion and that my preference (which is, I'm sure, shared by the majority of silent readers) for remaining incognito, invisible, be respected. I want to be able to come and go as I please, in full safety, without constantly running the risk of being harangued by some malicious watchman posted at the threshold to the domain into which, full of hope, I am preparing to make my entrance.

Nonetheless, I would have been inclined to overlook this initial awkwardness, to attribute it to some lack of delicacy (these days, you have to put up with that sort of thing if you want to continue to associate with people), had the content of the page itself not increased my uneasiness.

How should this kind of address be interpreted?

It could only be a joke. A wink, a little heavy-handed, toward a thundering Jarryesque outburst. Or perhaps, even more simply, a farce. Yes, as subtle, and in at least as good taste, as the old graffito that has delighted generations of schoolchildren. They hardly know how to write before it becomes their favorite thing to do. I can testify to this myself, for in certain neighborhoods in the suburb where I was born – not necessarily the most impoverished (in those neighborhoods, nobody was interested in writing, even on walls) – you saw it everywhere: inside buildings, hastily scribbled on the smooth walls of elevators or public toilets; outside, carved on the wooden fences around construction sites where the workers were on strike, or on the walls of buildings that were to be demolished. Every available surface was decorated with it. Amid the tediously repeated obscenities that explicitly exhibit, thanks to the convenience of anonymity, what our culture normally pretends not to know or tries to repress, one was sure to find it. Simultaneously a rallying cry for a few groups of outsiders and a vengeful manifesto exhaling wholesale anger, impatience, scorn. Sometimes ostentatious and provocative, with big, angular capital letters, sometimes written more cursively, discreetly and almost furtively, the message shone by its masculine concision: it was, largely inspired by the famous interjection (in four letters, just like the word 'book') of a famous imperial general, an energetic, flat refusal addressed to anyone who reads it.

On the whole, I'm not opposed to jokes. I am even prepared to recognize, as people used to do, that laughter has a sacred value, and I cannot forget that amid the ruins of Sparta, one stela survived all the others, the one that was dedicated to the god of Laughter. Better yet: if from the whole of contemporary intellectual production in every genre only a dozen good jokes (the kind that make you laugh the hundredth time you hear them) were to remain, I should think our generation had not lived in vain. That shows how good an audience I am. So why shouldn't I pardon my author, who was no doubt carried away by a whiff of childhood or nostalgia, this regression toward bathroom humor?

8

But what about the prophetic tone? And the ironic or condescending allusions to my expectations, my illusions? And, to crown it all, the desire to intimidate me, relying on barely veiled threats? All of that constitutes an apparatus that doesn't seem to have been intended simply as a pretext for clowning around.

I thought I was pretty capable of recognizing a scribbler's whims and fancies, and had been for a long time. I was aware in particular of the importance (excessive, to be sure, but this is not the place to go into it) that some people lay on safeguarding their family's recipes, their club's gossip, their clique's teeny secrets, which they seek to conceal from common, profane eyes. I would therefore have acknowledged without difficulty that certain precautions might have been taken with regard to me, that I might be snubbed a little bit, and even that I might be scolded. But in all my experience as an avid reader, which is always conveniently present to my memory (and heavily, sometimes!) at the moment that I begin a new book, I could find no example of a such an abrupt reception. Before telling Nathaniel to *dump the book*, damn it, one could at least wait until he'd finished reading it!

However, I had read about these hussar-like attacks, these insolent approaches, these overtures as imperious as they were impertinent, to which we impenitent readers used to be regularly treated.

I also remembered some of the famous *addresses to the reader* that formerly constituted, at the beginning of works presenting themselves as difficult or innovative, so many warnings. 'Timid soul, set your heels backward, not forward,' the anonymous author of the *Chants de Maldoror* once somewhat rudely advised. He was not the only one, nor even the first: another unknown author, a certain Alcofribas, long before . . . Even in these cases, which have become more or less classic (since their scandalous nature, which was originally very striking, has with time

9

become attenuated, as usual), the reader was always immediately provided with precise instructions, not to say threats, concerning the proper way of approaching the book. For one of these authors, the book was a box (or a bottle) that one had to learn how to open in order to grasp its precious contents; for the other, it was a bone that had to broken open in order to suck out its marrow.

This case was entirely different. The odd introductory remark looked very much like a prohibition. The exordium, instead of offering me brotherly guidance encouraging me not to give up too quickly when confronted by the difficulties to come, sought explicitly to exclude me, to exile me, in the most expeditious manner possible: I expected to be welcomed as a guest, and I found myself treated as an enemy. But the author, still more vicious than the ancient Barbarians who, bidding an ultimate farewell to the lands they had devastated, poisoned the springs and wells, chose to express his venom at the outset. In him, no trace of the kind of generosity that leads you to do the best you can in return. Like the cherub with the flaming sword who was to keep undesirables out of paradise, he thus established, between his work and me, an irremediable discontinuity. As if he wanted to perform all alone a ceremony to which he did not deem me worthy of being invited.

Perhaps the most unbearable thing about this guy was that he addressed me with such condescension (what right did he think he had to speak to me, right from the start, in such familiar terms?), as if I were a child. First of all, he reminded me, very inopportunely, of the time when my mother, worried (and no doubt secretly annoyed) to see me spending whole days confined to my room, staring into space, suggested – with an insistence that irritated me without persuading me – that I join my playmates outside in the sun and open air. Worse yet, he already claimed to know all my hopes and expectations and threw them in my face as if they were baseless dreams. Playing the prophet, he warned me against myself, acted as though he knew all the hidden corners of my mind and could read them as he would a book he had long ago deciphered.

Clearly, no one had ever treated me with such a mixture of arrogance and carelessness!

I refused (and who could blame me?) to pursue my reading any further.

'You ordered me to put this book down. Well, all right. I'm going to obey. Even better than you hoped. I'd be pretty stupid, after all, not to take you at your word.

'Do you have any idea how absurd you've been? Would you agree, except perhaps in the middle of some kind of nightmare, to hang around an artist's studio where you were allowed to enter and then immediately told to get out or close your eyes?

'To be sure, like those saints who are more eager for blame than praise, you are practicing an art of which I personally prefer to remain ignorant, the noble art of making enemies. Whom do you want to read you? God himself, maybe? Unless, like Baudelaire, you prefer to write for the dead . . .

'However that may be, you should know that your expectations are a matter of indifference to me. So stay in the company you've chosen. And if you want your work to be a mere soliloquy, go right ahead!

'On that note, Mr. Cerberus, I bid you good evening!'

Now *there*, I said to myself with intense satisfaction while I was silently scolding the impertinent author, is a particularly dignified exit, and one not without a certain panache.

This boor probably imagined that he could push me around

with impunity! By dismissing him myself, firmly and definitively, without a minute's hesitation, hadn't I succeeded in turning to my advantage a situation initially unfavorable to me, one that even threatened to become truly uncomfortable? Damn it, in literature these days, opportunities like that don't come along very often, especially for people like me, who are not much inclined to seek them out, so you have to know how to grab them when they come up.

And then, another consideration added to my satisfaction. It was connected with the inexhaustible tangle of memories that I usually try to keep dormant, but which my haranguer, in his thoughtlessness, had just stupidly awakened.

As I child, I learned that to be sure I always acted properly, all I had to do was to observe a few simple rules, which could be reduced to a very small number, at most a dozen, phrased in inalterable, lapidary formulas, austere in tone, piously transmitted in my family for many generations, and whose possession I considered a genuine talisman. They came straight out of the quietly ironic wisdom (itself ultimately optimistic) that all kinds of outsiders and minorities create to safeguard their image and to comfort their self-esteem, and they had quite naturally replaced the little treasury of nursery rhymes, proverbs, and maxims that up to then had helped get me out of all sorts of scrapes.

From both of these I had at least drawn a reassuring certainty: the world was not so terrible a thing as it appeared to be; one could, by using certain well-placed, well-chosen words, keep its most dangerous threats at a safe distance.

My experience as an adult had, of course, severely tested this ancient faith, without being able to destroy it (can one ever really destroy an edifice with such foundations?). In particular, I discovered the distance that separates the fine, harmonious, and rigid order that I had been taught to respect from the fleeting, unpredictable pulverulence of the reality I encountered every day. Therefore I was not sorry that I could still appeal, now and then, to one or another of these precious commandments.

There was one in particular, a genuine oracle, that had seemed to me worthy of the subtlest moralists, and which I kept in reserve, knowing that someday it would come to my aid and help me save face. That day had finally come. I was going to test immediately the pertinence and efficacy of my formula: *If someone keeps me at a distance,* I had often heard my mother say (for in the closed world in which we lived, there was no lack of opportunities to say it, or at least to think it), *my consolation is that he keeps his distance too.*

So without delay, I closed the volume: I'd had enough problems for that day.

2

Furem signata sollicitant. Aperta effractarius praeterit.
— Seneca

B y the way, did I mention that that day was a Sunday, that it was my fortieth birthday, and that, in the dark, cluttered room which, because my new lodgings are very cramped (a crummy furnished apartment I had had a hard time finding, on the dividing line between the nineteenth and the twentieth arrondissements), serves as my office, library, and even, on occasion (thanks to a tired old leather couch left behind by an earlier tenant), as a guest room, I was tidying up?

A special moment: only a Sunday, soaked from the outset in the perfume of fresh sheets and Earl Grey tea, really lends itself to this kind of work, which is never completed. What others consider an unrewarding task (the hostility with which some of my woman friends talked, a few years ago, about the bourgeois need to tidy up!) I had gradually succeeded in turning into one of my favorite pleasures. For years, in the various places that chance has led me to choose (always provisionally) as my domicile, I have engaged in this task with regularity and delight. I have always had a weakness for order. Moreover, this periodic exercise sometimes yielded very pleasant surprises.

For example, just the preceding week I had rediscovered, stuck between two big notebooks bound in black cloth (that's where I write down the most striking passages found in my reading), Emma's last letter. Sweet Emma . . . We had grown up together. Of all my little cousins, she was the one I got along with best: she had such soft, white breasts! And though we dared not become lovers, being excessively well-behaved adolescents, we caressed each other furtively and at length, on Saturday evenings, hidden in the tall grass behind the crumbling wall of the old cemetery. At that time we dreamed of running away to Constantinople, which of course we never did. Instead, several years later, the poor girl had to follow her doctor-husband to a small town in Normandy. A few months earlier, we had begun corresponding again; Emma told me which contemporary novels to read, her taste and her situation leading her to read more of them than I did. Folded twice, and scribbled as usual on the back of a blank prescription form, this precious missive (containing a short list of books I *must* read) had gotten lost during my move, before I had even had time to open it.

But that Sunday, my rummaging about had not produced anything miraculous. None of those surprises that illuminate. The chaos of my office remained more or less sterile. At most I noted, without any particular pleasure, the sudden reappearance of an old spiral notebook forgotten long ago: in it were copied some of the observations, always concise and judicious, that an old family friend of indefatigable fidelity had thought it necessary to send me, year after year, in his dispatches from Rouen.

The truth is (it's time I admitted this) that I wasn't in the best of shape.

First, because my sleep the previous night had been – to put the best face on it – both short and fitful. I was not to blame for this. On the contrary. I had gone to bed early, something I rarely do, and which in any case I had not done for a long time. But I had several times been awakened with a start by a whole series of unusual noises (slamming doors, more or less stifled sobs, outbursts) that stopped only to begin again a few moments later. My upstairs neighbors' marital spats, which had become frequent, had never been so violent and lengthy. This one ended only at dawn, with the prolonged creaking and groaning of a bed usually subjected to less frenetic, more discreet punishment.

Moreover, I'd been distracted ever since I woke up. For weeks my days had been spent mainly in endless ruminations on Sophie's acts, gestures, and supposed intentions.

Where was she? With whom? What was she doing? Would she come? At what time? Would she stay? How long? Would we finally be able to resolve our differences, or at least arrive at an understanding? Such were the thoughts that were pounding through my head as I shifted about, without conviction or attention, and without even incessant whistling (the same old air by Purcell, *Come, come, ye sons of art*, had accompanied these activities for years), the piles of books and boxes overflowing with files and manuscripts.

I tried to imagine how our evening together would go. My fortieth birthday! Sophie could not let me spend it alone: she was too aware of what that date meant to me. Nevertheless, I had forced myself not to prepare anything special for the occasion. I just wanted to be available, ready to satisfy unhesitatingly every one of her wishes.

No doubt she would arrive late (that was her habit): not before midnight. And she would be radiant. As on the day we first met. A meeting whose every moment I never ceased to relive in my imagination, marveling more each time (so such a thing had actually happened to me, to me!).

There had been a party that night, at my friend Marc's place. Just before leaving for Bali, he had invited his 'pals' (at least a hundred) for one of his usual little get-togethers. That was what we called these soirées, of which he was both organizer and hero, and which he had been able to turn into an indispensable institution. They were certainly not the unbridled bacchanalia that some people, filled with nostalgia for the great moments of exuberant elation they had experienced elsewhere (*Ah! the great meetings in front of the cathedral, in Havana, with their extravagant stage-setting, speech after speech, songs, bands . . .*) would have liked them to be; but you were at least sure to find there almost everyone whom, for good reasons or bad, you had not gotten around to seeing for the past few months.

It was not long past midnight. In every corner of the apartment, there was a sort of joyful chaos. All kinds of bottles were making the rounds. Little glasses (and others, of less limited dimensions) were being filled, and there were cigarette butts and half-empty bottles in the most unexpected places.

The narrow terrace, brilliantly lighted, was jammed with people: Marc, taking advantage of the exceptionally warm weather, had put the buffet out there. The buzz of conversation did not succeed in drowning out the booming music.

In the main room, where two large candles were burning, a few couples, clinging tightly to each other, pretended to dance. I watched them with indifference. All that was beginning to seem to me very far away: I had arrived at the age when dancing is no longer pleasure or pretext, but only fatiguing. Other people, silhouettes suddenly emerging from the shadows, difficult to identify, bounded past with bursts of laughter.

A small group, which I ended up joining, had taken refuge in the bedroom: about a dozen people, more or less jammed in. In the middle: Gouggenheim, lying propped against the bedposts, his hands clutching a couple of handwritten pages he never took his eyes off. For a quarter of an hour he had been declaiming the first pages of a short story that he had found, he told us, very difficult to complete (and since we had long known about his tumultuous relations with literary matters, we were sure that this was not mere affectation).

Everyone was silent, attentive. The text was not easy. And the sound coming from the other rooms sometimes made it hard to hear. Actually, I'd been annoyed by the puzzling tone of the beginning. It was the story of a young man, really quite passionate, who had set out to reconstitute the various animal languages, and had undertaken for this purpose a long and arduous journey. But I felt much more comfortable with the last fragment, a buoyant love song in authentic gorilla language.

Suddenly, right in the middle of the refrain, Gouggenheim, who for the first time had lifted his eyes to look at his audience, began to stutter, blushed furiously, and stopped dead. A woman, clearly unknown to him and to the rest of those present, had just come into the room.

She was dazzling. I'd been so dazzled only once before, when I was eighteen, and had often wondered whether I would ever experience anything like that again, except in books.

Sophie, for it was she, didn't look like anyone I had ever seen before, except perhaps in a few Indian paintings of an earlier age, or in certain Persian miniatures: tall and very slender, with long, black hair, her skin and eyes a color that no word in our language can render (certain kinds of honey, and perhaps some very old cognacs, might render it very imperfectly), and features of an almost incredible refinement.

It all happened immediately, as soon as we were introduced. We were facing each other. Our knees were almost touching. Smiling, she held out her hand and repeated my name, which took on in her mouth a sweetness it had not had for a long time. I hardly heard her name, and remained silent. I had to close my eyes again for a few seconds. The helpless look I gave her when she touched me could have been my perdition. But she responded with an even brighter smile. I recovered my breath. I was able to speak again.

I haven't the faintest idea what I said.

19

We soon withdrew to the only dark corner of the terrace, and on our way there I overturned, in my haste, two or three glasses that had been left on the floor. From that moment, as if a moat had been dug around us, no one dared disturb us. Before long, the night had dissolved all the obstacles separating us, and erased all the difficulties.

In the wee hours of the morning, our arms around each other, and under the surprised gaze (in which, however, there was also a bit of admiration) of Marc and the last guests still present, who had gathered in the kitchen around the traditional dish of spaghetti *al burro*, we left the party. And during the following days (it was one of those long weekends that in certain years the calendar, in its generosity, bestows on us in profusion), we were never separated.

Three days and three nights. Outside time and space.

Sophie had immediately accepted my love. She had perceived it, she said, at the very moment of its birth. And to do so she had needed no word, no appeal other than my first glance.

As for me . . . Something that had been dormant for years suddenly awakened. During these few days, my whole horizon was redefined around her. A word – the most unexpected, the most precise – was all she needed to strip the most banal things of their veneer of convention, to restore their original brilliance and strangeness. Up to that point, I had believed, on the basis of a few unhappy experiences, that the world of women was irremediably divided into two groups: those who produced pleasure, and those who produced dreams; I discovered how wrong I had been. I felt that I was about to escape from the circle of boredom and anxiety, that I would finally begin to live.

After this miraculous start, alas, things had taken a less glorious turn. And I hoped this day would mark the beginning of a new era.

So it was hard to wait, almost unbearable.

This unknown volume had suddenly appeared in my hands, and I was intrigued by its look. Thin, almost flat, and oblong in format, it scarcely resembled the weighty tomes that usually cluttered my work table.

As a matter of fact, I don't like books whose size or weight are much out of the ordinary. As far back as I can remember, I see myself always dealing with this kind of object: I could hardly read and already I was piling them up next to my bed; some mornings, when it was time to go to school, I even struggled to stuff a couple of them into my fragile leatherette briefcase. It was then that I acquired a taste for big dictionaries (in fifteen, seventeen, or twenty-one volumes, with the complete series of annual supplements if possible), encyclopedias (especially when they had dozens of volumes of engraved plates), catalogues (often full of color reproductions and facsimiles) – in short, for every kind of *corpus,* into which I dived with voluptuous pleasure, pencil in hand.

With their long columns, tightly packed lines, and miniscule letters, they no doubt greatly contributed to the ruination of my eyesight (attested by the thickness of my lenses), but at least they helped me satisfy my inveterate taste for exhaustive inventories, my need to classify, to count, to organize, to list.

How did it happen to slip in among my books, this intruder that was obviously out of place? Clearly, someone had put it there. But who? I no longer had many visitors: my persistent gloom had pretty much discouraged some of my friends. In any case, since my last tidying-up, no one had come into my office (except for Sophie, of course, and even she did so rarely, because she didn't like this room almost without daylight).

I was about to put the book back on the pile from which I had taken it. I was rejoicing *in petto* at the time I was going to gain by so quickly breaking off my reading. I even congratulated myself on not having, that day (by what obscure prescience?) proceeded as I usually did. My habit is in fact never to begin a book with the first page, which is always too enticing for my taste. I don't like to allow myself to be obliged to follow an immutable path, as if we were still in the time when the ancient parchment scroll had to be unrolled bit by bit, column by column. On the contrary, I like to take my time and scout out a new book. I feel it. I smell it (someone should write a whole treatise on the smells of books, which are so various, so precise: the smells of different papers, which occasionally seem to have absorbed some of the scents of their distant countries of origin, the smells of the inks, with lingering odors of blood flowing back in, and, of course, the smells of the countless leathers used for the bindings). I leaf through it. Then I skim it for a long time, picking out here and there certain sentences, or more often certain words, that speak to me: the word *word*, like the word *read* and the word *said* never fail (unlike the word *street* or the word *late*) to catch my eye. This ceremony takes time, but at least it reassures me: I always know what I have to expect, if I decide, now or later, to begin a real reading, which then cannot be interrupted for any reason.

But before saying farewell to it, a farewell that would probably be definitive (for who knows when chance might thrust such an impertinent book back into my hands?), I wanted to examine it (oh, just briefly) more closely: in fact, truly separating myself from a book, even a bad one (but how can one be sure that a book is irremediably bad as long as one has not explored its every recess?), is a rupture I find difficult to bear.

Two unusual details, which I was astonished not to have noticed right away, struck me.

First, the absence, in the places normally reserved for it, of the author's name: neither on the spine, nor on the front cover, not even inside, on the title page. All I could discover – not without difficulty, for these clues had become almost illegible because of a large, dark stain – was that book had been *printed*, on an unspecified date, *by the Martial Press, Aubenas*. Defying tradition, the author had refused to take the risk of identifying himself, and his work thus had all the characteristics of anonymity. This seemed to me extremely disagreeable: I like to know who is talking to me, especially when someone is taking leave of me. I therefore wondered what had led this fellow (the boor who had just enraged me) to conceal himself in this way. An odd man of letters, after all, who apparently was not one of those who dream of inscribing, through their work, their name on people's memories.

Nevertheless, I didn't want to overemphasize this point, despite its importance; I could always come back to it later on. Another peculiarity, still more unexpected, had just attracted my attention: the singular appearance of the title. It was not on the cover, either (the cover thus remaining completely mute), but stood out boldly on the first page, isolated, massive, indecipherable.

I was aware, of course, that most authors prefer titles that are obscure, ambiguous, even enigmatic, because they think them more likely to awaken the reader's curiosity (which is always, it has to be admitted, a little somnolent). I was even prepared to acknowledge that in this domain, they had come up, over the past few years, with some rather clever ones, as delightful in my view as some particularly successful crossword puzzle clues (one of my friends collected these and sent them to me as he discovered them). But this was something entirely different: I was unable to decipher a title that lay right before my eyes. Or rather, unable to identify the origin of the letters that had been used in composing it! Exactly as if I had become illiterate!

This had happened to me very rarely in my life, and even then it was under exceptional circumstances: the first time, long ago, in one of those 'country inns' with shimmering copperware, when the maître d', dressed entirely in black, ceremoniously spread out before my schoolboy eyes, intimidated by his enormous white mustache, a voluminous menu written entirely in gothic letters; or again, more recently, when my friend Flauzac sent me some of his articles in Japanese translation.

I was seized by doubt, and things seemed to me much less clear than they had at the outset. An opening address that rudely dismisses the unfortunate reader, an author who dares not say his name, a title that does not allow itself to be read: the accumulation of anomalies was becoming disturbing. And a question could not fail to arise: was I right to react so brutally to the page I had read a little while ago?

Could an informed reader (and what claim did I have in this world other than to be that kind of reader, careful not to miss anything, aware of the beauties and risks inherent in his favorite activity?) just take a text for what it appeared to be? Was it legitimate to believe to that extent in the transparency of language and writers' sincerity? These days, that kind of naïveté is no longer acceptable. The first schoolboy who comes along (assuming, of course, that he has been well taught by his masters) knows that you have to go beyond the literal meaning to track down the allusion.

And then, I was certainly not going to acquiesce, on the pretext that it had been exercised by the author himself, in what amounted to nothing less than a kind of censorship! What good would so much reading have done me if I were to obey orders like some rustic, to abdicate my freedom of judgment, in short to allow my attitude to be dictated by a stranger? Damn it, I finally said to myself, it's high time to remember that the secret of reading lies, if anywhere, in rebellion rather than in allegiance!

I was therefore determined to be exceptionally vigilant, to draw no conclusions without careful reflection, and certainly not without a degree of circumspection. Indeed, I would repeat to myself, like a litany, that forms are mobile, that there are no immutable criteria of beauty, and not let myself be buffaloed by something that seemed alien. The latter might be (can we ever be sure in these eminently versatile times?) only the index of a fashion. A fashion of which I was not yet aware, either because it had been too ephemeral to have had the time to reach me, in spite of the efforts I make to keep up to date, or on the contrary, because it was still emerging.

It was at this point that an intuition struck me. One of those violent intuitions that descend on you under the most unexpected circumstances. This usually happens when you're very far from home, in places that seem to have their own time and space: in the small, gilded parlor of a villa on the coast of Carthage, when everything is permeated by the scent of orange blossoms; a Christmas day in an almost empty 757 at high altitude, under a radiant noonday sun, flying over the Nevada desert; at the entrance to a long tunnel, in the ill-lit compartment of a night train crossing, at a snail's pace, the snowy Appenines, between Nocera and Nardi. It was difficult, as I well knew, to resist such sudden apparitions, so strongly do they compel belief. For just a few seconds, our mental faculties seem to gain increased power, and the mind is dazzled by a brilliant light.

It's clear, I said to myself, *I must be dealing with a text far more complex than it seems. A text in which seven references can be concealed behind every word, nine sources behind every sentence. One of those texts so full of allegories that they allow the reader only too great a choice of interpretations, and that therefore have to be taken at the second, or perhaps the third (indeed, who knows, even at the fourth . . .) degree.*

I had many reasons for taking an interest in this kind of work, which satisfied some of my old penchants that had long remained unavowed. First of all, hidden somewhere deep in my brain, there was a sort of nostalgia: the hope of seeing the meaning of things revealed once again in its old clarity. Then there was the certainty, more recently acquired, that I had entered into that time of life in which everything suddenly becomes a warning. But above all there was the feeling, which paradoxically complemented the others, that the truth (insofar as there is anything that corresponds to that word) is marked particularly by the care with which it conceals itself.

And what if this fellow belonged, I thought, *precisely to that category of puzzle-makers who, like meticulous lawyers, cultivate a kind of hermetism and do not hesitate to employ ruses in order to deliver mysterious or amusing messages?*

There was nothing extravagant about that hypothesis.

For I now remembered the probable circumstances under which I had acquired this book. These were somewhat unusual: it belonged, I thought, to the little batch of books that had been sold to me, for next to nothing, by one of my former fellow-students, who, short of money after serious disappointments in publishing, was now selling books at the end of the boulevard Bourdon, where it is crossed by the rue Davout, in Bourges.

3

For years, my friend's fate had constantly provided me with cause for worry (it is true that I am rather easily worried when those dear to me are concerned) and a subject for meditation (I admit that I have an irrepressible penchant for meditation: a trifle plunges me into it, and afterward nothing can get me out of it again). For Monsieur Gustave de Flauzac was no ordinary person. Would you mind very much if I told you at least a little of his story?

Flauzac did not like to talk about his origins: *I am not,* he said, *one of those who move forward by using their family as a shield.* Nonetheless, his life had been strongly influenced by his family, more than he let show, though he would not have wanted to acknowledge it. By doing some cross-checking, I had been able to discover that he was the product of a very romantic (but totally unpredictable) union. His parents, whom I liked to imagine as young, attractive, and madly in love, had not hesitated to get married secretly, against the will of both their families. These families were a heavy burden: Coming straight out of old provincial society, which was pretty rigid, and still imbued with the preceding century's pride and prejudices. On one side, they were well-off Rouen bourgeois whose money came from the practice of surgery; on the other, minor, rather impoverished nobles from Tours: the former, who rejected the notion that one might act on the basis of something as illusory and transitory as feeling, had seen this marriage as a mistake and a serious violation of the rules under which they had been brought up; the latter, less inhuman in their disapproval, thought it merely a bit of youthful nonsense that wouldn't last long. Strains, conflicts, ruptures, flight: the young people, who had had too much, ended up making their home far away from their troublesome parents, in Bourges. It was there that Gustave was brought up.

He was five years old when his first teacher, who did not like him because he smelled too much, told him, to mock him one day when he had failed to distinguish a 'p' from a 'q,' *You'll never learn how to read*. From that day on, encouraged by his parents, who devoted virtually all their time and attention to him, he had specialized in deciphering, and had learned, as if to amuse himself, almost all the alphabets in the world.

Then, quite naturally, he went to Paris. Surrounded by the aura of the academic prize he had easily won (at the university, the least of his efforts met with enthusiastic praise), he had soon made a special place for himself in the little group to which I belonged.

With his athletic build (he was a good head taller than any of us, which always obliged him to bend over a bit), his prematurely gray beard, and his eyes of the sweetest blue, he charmed us all. But he also impressed us: endowed with what seemed a limitless capacity for work and devoured by an unbridled thirst for knowledge, he was born to be a kind of encyclopedist. And that was what he became. I can testify to the fact that his early years were spent reading a long succession of more or less learned books, which he excitedly told us about in sessions where his search for the right word, the right expression, sometimes made him seem pedantic to the less indulgent among us.

He allowed himself only a few minor ancillary activities, concerning which he was perfectly discreet (he was never very good at confiding salacious secrets). For example, he accorded an important place to letters, and everyone knew that he must not be disturbed when he withdrew to *catch up on his correspondence*. This delicate operation, which was repeated every week, seemed to absorb most of his affective life, for in this domain, despite appearances, he was more like Cherubin than Don Juan (but a Cherubin less martial than sensual). Therefore he carried on romantic and epistolary love affairs with a series of exotic, rather pretentious young women (we always wondered where and how he met them, for he hardly ever left his studio, whose windows were always closed). Some of these women occasionally surprised him, on a fine May or October day, by showing up at his door, smiling and carrying a suitcase. They never stayed very long.

People always told him – and this was only too obvious for those who, like myself, had had the good fortune (sometimes) to receive letters from him, or to hear him (rarely) read passages from the *Diary* he didn't like to talk about – that he had what it takes to make a writer. This observation, especially if it came from a friend, annoyed him; it clearly touched a sore point. Nevertheless, he replied. Sometimes by complex, voluble, learned discourses, in which various famous names never failed to recur: Virgil, Gogol, Kafka.

But usually he limited himself to quips, which he varied according to his mood. Did he feel like being ironic? That could produce: *The right stuff to make a writer, yes, but it's not a good idea to make a suit for yourself with that stuff,* sometimes reduced to *a stuff from which you can never make more than a jacket.* Bitter? *You never really finish a book; why begin one?* Playful? *I see no difference between dreaming a book and writing one. Besides, a true book pokes fun at books.* Disillusioned? *A lover of words is never at a loss for a good reason to keep his trap shut.* You never knew how to take these remarks.

However, I myself had certain ideas concerning the reasons for this malaise. Not that he had ever given me an explanation; with me, his last word on the subject was invariably: *I have always felt sufficiently mature to remain silent, that's all.* In fact, these ideas had come to me in the course of our lengthy work sessions: long hours spent thinking together, whose memory still remains dear to my heart. For although he didn't care for what he called with a smile 'group textuality,' Flauzac – who never acknowledged any ambition other than collective ones – simply practiced it. With me, he was particularly fond of reviving the most ancient arguments. He settled them by means of quotations he didn't take the trouble to translate. The whole history of arts and letters passed in review, and he saw in it only a long series of ambiguities, hesitations, pentimenti, and dead ends . . .

Thus I had had an opportunity to note the frequency of his sarcastic remarks about those who, because they are incapable of writing an article or a short story (with all that these presuppose in the way of concision, rigor, and precision), give up and write a book, or even several books. Rightly or wrongly, it seemed to me that I had also discerned a confession in a comment that escaped him one day when he was having a particularly animated discussion with Mathieu. He felt very sorry, he said, for those whose *obsession with writing had ended up devouring all their time for reading.* In fact, he was one of those for whom reading is neither a pleasure nor a pastime, but a vocation – the only vocation, so to speak.

Nevertheless, I could not help thinking that he was the victim of an absurd fashion and imagining what his fate might have been a century earlier. Endowed with the kind of knowledge he had acquired, he would have left for some country in the Near or Far East. There, for several years, working with a team of native laborers totally devoted to him, he would have indulged in the wildest speculations on the basis of the ancient, precious documents he had the good luck to dig up and the patience to decipher. Back in Paris, he would have straightaway published, together with many plates and engraved maps, the results of his research, which would have won him the immediate and enduring esteem of all men of letters. Then, through assiduous work, he would have ended up being appointed to a chair at the Collège de France, or in the Académie des Inscriptions, or perhaps both.

Instead, he had withdrawn into his refusal to write as if into a stronghold, being well aware that he would cease to be invulnerable if he someday committed the error of emerging from it.

However, he had decided, to my great surprise, to become a publisher. Not in order to encourage, by publishing new books, a malignant proliferation that sickened him. But rather, on the contrary, to try, indirectly, to restrain it. Thus he specialized, as some people surely still recall, in rediscovering forgotten authors, neglected works. His instinct and learning quickly produced marvels. He had succeeded in bringing back to light numerous masterpieces whose authors' excessive discretion had kept in unjust obscurity and that had not yet had the benefit, among later generations, of the increased visibility they deserved. A large audience, which thereby discovered the existence of another literary world, acquired the habit of buying the few new volumes, very carefully produced under their pale green jackets, that Flauzac brought out each trimester. Very soon, *L'Herbe Tendre*, the business he had created, was flourishing: it left its remote location in the rue des Flots (an odd, low building, long and narrow, with a veranda and a small garden full of roses, with clematis in the middle) in order to be set up in a noble, tranquil edifice a stone's throw from the towers of Saint-Sulpice. Naturally, this success won Flauzac some serious enemies in publishing circles. But completely absorbed by his discoverer's passion, ready to sacrifice to this passion the small successes that a benevolent fate had conferred upon him in

31

abundance, he dreamed only of realizing what was, in his view, his life work. A grandiose project that concerned all the world's literatures, and for which he had to recruit hundreds of collaborators, handsomely remunerated, in every country. In a short time, he was ruined. He then returned to Bourges, where he lived for months as a recluse.

When he finally began to get back on his feet, the problem of his future resurfaced: since it was clear that there was no question of giving up books, of abandoning his conversation with literature, what was he to do?

For a time, he thought about opening a reading room, like the one he had sometimes frequented as a child, in a side lane off the Galerie Vivienne, and whose memory haunted him without his knowing why. Day after day, amid overloaded bookshelves and little round tables covered with green velvet, he would have used his knowledge, kindly but firmly, to direct toward the highest summits of universal literature the erratic curiosity of a small band of faithful subscribers, whose tireless Pygmalion he would be. For their benefit, he would have organized, several times a month, evening readings: he would have put on, for the occasion, his handsome black suit, his velvet toque adorned with a golden tassel, and during his reading, he would not have failed to perceive (for the excess of his misfortune had not altered his lovely, candid eyes) the devoted glances of his most faithful female auditors.

He was dissuaded from embarking upon this project. Not without difficulty.

Fate would have it that at this point he saw a classified ad that allowed him to rent for next to nothing a former bakery, which he had, by patching it up here and there, transformed into a warehouse for his books.

This place, which, when he set himself up in it, looked for all the world like a dive (and was, for this reason, still avoided by the 'good society' of Bourges), had a singular appearance: it was literally crammed, from floor to ceiling, with thousands of books, not organized in any way. These books were not, as is usual, arranged on shelves (the shelves being, in this case, simply non-existent), but piled up in teetering columns, among which, if you didn't want to find yourself suddenly buried in a kind of avalanche, you had to walk very carefully. These were the last vestiges of the glorious period, which the bailiffs and creditors (who were not, fortunately, knowledgeable in such matters) had neglected to seize when Flauzac went bankrupt, considering them worthless. But the stock had become still larger with the arrival (unexpectedly and by the dozens) of enormous cartons full of small bound volumes (in precious romantic bindings) from the legacy of Flauzac's grandmother in Rouen. The shop's disorder had now become so great that it was necessary to create, in order to display these new treasures, an annex. Then Flauzac conceived the idea of using the old baker's oven, a vast, dark basement which could be reached only through a longish tunnel, so narrow that you couldn't walk through it two abreast.

In this sort of grotto he had collected the books that he did not wish to display. He liked to go down there by himself, at first, as if to a religious site; he sometimes remained there for hours (hours that seemed to him as long and full as genuine days), tête-à-tête with some of the heroes he gathered around him by opening the story of their adventures, heroes who immediately took complete possession of his person. When he emerged from this retreat and saw the light of day, he had a hard time keeping his eyes open, and although he was in the most familiar surroundings, he walked like a man who is having difficulty finding his way.

What use could he make of his singular collection of books? The question strongly preoccupied our friend.

We knew that with each of these volumes he had, for many years (in some cases, since his childhood), maintained a relationship of affectionate familiarity; he knew each book's author and date of publication, and he could summarize its content on the spot, while at the same time describing the weather on the day when he had opened it for the first time. Therefore he would consider only with revulsion the idea of dispersing them or getting along without them.

However, several of us suggested that he make, if not a complete inventory (that would have taken months), at least a catalog of the most precious items – many booksellers would have taken delight in perusing it.

He set himself to the task. We had to help him. It was a real trial for him.

To be sure, it allowed him to find texts that probably had never, since their publication, had any reader other than him. But above all, it forced him to observe the deterioration of some of his books. He was distraught each time he lovingly picked up one of these volumes that he considered an extension of himself, only to discover its infirmities: worn corners or edges, cracked spines, browning, stains on the pages, yellowing plates, traces of dampness, missing clasps, wormholes. After a few weeks, overwhelmed, he gave up.

But the idea of separating himself from some of his books had made some headway. Suddenly, he made up his mind. Getting out his beloved sign of the *Herbe Tendre*, he transformed his warehouse into a shop, which he opened to the public. But it has to be said that most of these books were hardly likely to interest the unfortunate customers who happened to come in on certain days. For this chapel had not yet found the worshipers it deserved and had to be satisfied with a clientele that was as small as it was various. In the darkness of winter afternoons, around four o'clock, retired postal workers, high school students with flat shoes and round glasses, along with housewives carrying their shopping baskets, rubbed elbows without noticing each other, and left again empty-handed after having wandered about for a long time amid the fragile columns of paper. However, once, in the middle of August, a Japanese man with an adolescent face got out of a big gray car and went away again with a smile on his lips, carrying an English copy of Poe's *Aphorisms* that Maurice Sachs had annotated during his involuntary stay in the Fuhlsbüttel prison near Hamburg.

Thus Gustave had decided to make a different use of at least part of his treasure-trove. He acquired the habit of quite regularly selecting a few items, those that seemed to him to deserve a better fate than the slow rot that inevitably awaited them in Bourges, in order to give them (the more or less symbolic sum that he sometimes agreed to accept in exchange did not allow these transactions to be called sales) to friends who were passing through. A sacrifice that he now justified with the formula: 'I should have derived little benefit from my books if I didn't know how to lose them.' But perhaps this was also only a way of maintaining, and rewarding, certain fidelities that might have proven less assiduous without this attraction.

With an almost miraculous instinct, he was able to divine what was likely to please each person, and we never had cause to complain about his choices or his suggestions. I less than anyone else. For I regarded him as an oracle, and owed to him many of the treasures of my library.

Thanks to him, I was able to acquire the last masterpiece written by Hugh Vereker (one of the many authors to whom he had introduced me), *Right of Passage*. But especially, it was Flauzac who dug up for me, and gave me (recommending, with an imperative smile, that I not let them go for any reason), copies of the sole edition (pulped during the war at the German authorities' command) of the twin novels (*Bearskin* and *Prey for Shadow*) by Mathias Flannery, an author previously unknown to me, and whose essay *The Gaze of Orpheus* had left me, when I read it, petrified with admiration.

Some of the moments of the afternoon we'd spent together came back to me.

It was a Sunday. A gentle rain had been falling since the morning. He was wearing a green oilskin coat when he met me at the door. His smile immediately reassured me. 'Ha, ha!' he could not help chortling as he bent down to greet me, 'that's the way I am, you see, rainy Sundays cheer me up . . . and make me feel younger!' And we immediately went toward his office, talking all the way. Our conversations were never burdened with preludes, they went right to the point. Our tête-à-tête followed the ritual pattern he had observed for years.

First of all, over a cup of tea (which he preferred lukewarm, whereas I drink it boiling hot), news about our mutual friends, with whom he maintained, as in the good old days, regular contacts: everything seemed to be going well in that area.

Then, very quickly, the eternal subject came up: books. This could last for hours.

That day, Flauzac, who always had some marvelous new discovery to show each of his visitors, took from a chest inlaid with ivory a very singular copy of the Talmud: its magnificent binding, in pigskin, made it strictly untouchable for those whom it would normally attract! Then he showered me with anecdotes, at least one of which I recall: the one about the typist who couldn't resist making very subtle (and very perverse) changes in the books entrusted to him . . .

I liked the volubility that allowed him, at such times, to assimilate everything and reproduce everything: 'It's nothing,' he would say, 'all you have to know is how to open the right drawer at the right time.'

Nonchalant and paradoxical, and sometimes slightly mocking (in the name of the grandeur of the 'ancients,' he was unfairly critical of almost all his contemporaries), but ultimately extremely indulgent, he tempered my enthusiasms with a smile, corrected my errors of judgment with a single word, expressed his astonishment at my ignorance (in all these areas, I usually kept him busy). But he was also capable, sometimes, of adopting a less self-assured tone; occasionally, he even doubted, and let me see it, for which I was grateful to him.

To bring the afternoon to an end, the walk (just as much a part of the ritual as all the rest: only the itinerary was subject to variations, which were, moreover, minor). Despite the persistent rain, we chose *the long walk*, which had led us, by way of Aleas Lane (normally prohibited to pedestrians at that hour), as far as the cathedral. Ever since he was a child, Flauzac had known every nook and cranny of the cathedral, and he never grew tired of walking through it, looking for memories. He had studied the relics one by one, reconstructed the history of each of the chapels, identified the subjects of all the stained glass windows. One of his favorite games was locating and naming the donors: In some cases, he explained to no one in particular, adopting for the occasion the bizarre lingo and staccato diction of a lecturer who is finding it difficult to read his notes, they were represented directly in the picture (in a privileged, significant place: for example, along a particular axis or at a special intersection), often presented by their patron saint, while in others they were indicated only by their coats of arms or by a detail still less evident to the vulgar eye. And it was always with greedy pleasure, and an air of personal triumph, that he revealed in what ways, subtle or indirect, the identity of the commissioner had nourished, in each case, the artist's creative expression.

On that day, leaving the stained glass windows behind, he had led me toward the tympanum over the door of the Last Judgment. It was his favorite. Once again, he dilated on the depiction of the resurrection of the dead: the figures' nudity and the extraordinary truth of the representation had always fascinated him.

We returned in silence. On the way, we stopped, long enough for me to catch my breath, in the middle of a pine grove that crawled up the hillside. Nothing had changed since the last time I had been there: the same hamlets covered with the same gray mist, which also covered the sky, the trees, and, farther on, a few houses and their little gardens.

After a modest supper (bean soup, a shoulder of beef, and a cream puff, which had been *his* dessert ever since he was a child), followed by rather prolonged farewells, I left him. I carried under my arm the package he had prepared for me, and which we had gone to fetch in the annex, taking the narrow, underground tunnel that led to it. It was a significantly heavier package than any of the preceding ones, and it was tied up with a string so thick and coarse that it surprised me: it lacked the delicacy I associated with my friend.

I didn't have time to ask Flauzac what was in this new package, and that was not in conformity with our usual habits. He only said to me, as he accompanied me to the end of the garden, in front of the iron gate that creaked so disagreeably when the evening wind slammed it, 'Oh, you'll see, you'll see. I think they're the kind of things you need just now. Remember: good books sterilize, they can't be equaled.' He added, after a moment of silence, 'And then, if you don't like these, you can always send them back to me. Separately or together . . .' I'd scarcely shut the gate before a tiny owl, nested in the nearby oak tree, grazed my face as he flew away.

That very evening, when I got home, I grabbed a knife and joyously cut the string, which turned out to be stronger than I had expected; then I unwrapped with difficulty the various layers of thick paper that protected the package, took out the volumes (there were, if I remember correctly, seven, or perhaps eight, of them), and very carefully wiped away the greasy black dirt encrusted on some of the brittle covers. Afterward, regretfully restraining my curiosity (I don't recall what alimentary task awaited me, and I had already been putting it off too long), I piled them on the far left corner of my desk, a sort of purgatory where my new acquisitions ended up while waiting to be made genuinely part of my library. For this is an operation that, in my case, cannot be lightly undertaken; it requires time and reflection.

I had adopted, on this subject, the opinion Marc had repeated countless times: *Books form a family*, he said; *a library is a living organism.* I even tried to apply this maxim literally. As I see it, the place occupied by a volume on a shelf is not a matter of indifference; it is determined by a highly complex set of factors (which are, moreover, subject to periodic change): these include, to be sure, elements such as the author's name, the subject or subjects dealt with, the format, the quality or rarity of the edition . . . But in fact, the most important considerations are clearly more subjective, and have to do with the degree of interest I take in the volume and the probable frequency with which I will use it. That is, a new book, before winning the right to fall into a long sleep in its definitive place, may be assigned, depending on my mood or needs, various residences, sometimes the least expected ones (on a shelf in the bathroom, under the couch in my office, or on top of the refrigerator in the kitchen).

A few months went by. Thanks to the autumn rains that had just arrived, along with their accompanying thunder and lightning, I had begun catching up on some of the things I'd put off. But I'd not had time to deal with the batch of books from Bourges, which I had not even made a serious attempt to inventory, and with which, despite my efforts, more recent acquisitions had been mixed.

This book, with its glacial exordium, was thus the first one I happened to pick off the pile: it couldn't be negligible or insignificant. The more I examined it, the more the hypothesis my intuition suggested – that a mystery was hidden in it somewhere – seemed likely to be confirmed.

I recalled that some time ago (and this had moreover surprised and amused me, coming from a man who did not precisely correspond, at least in my view, to the stereotype of the theosophist or alchemist) dear old Flauzac had acknowledged a weakness for cryptography and was even prepared, on occasion, to toy with occultism. To tell the truth, I don't know where he acquired this taste (for him, it was probably a way of forgetting his past misadventures), or how far he had gone along this path. I had been careful not to ask him any questions about the subject. Despite our close friendship, had I asked him, an ironic smile would have been his only response.

But I could testify to the fact that in what remained of his private library, which I knew well, as I know the libraries of all the people I care about (and who would undoubtedly be slightly less dear to me if I didn't know what books provided their daily nourishment), there were, collected and classified with great care, the works of Khalid and Fucanelli, Gouggenheim and Trithemius, Bosc, Vigenère and Villeneuve, Ambelain, Agapeyeff, and Jolliet, not to mention, of course (for it is the virtue of certain libraries that they allow authors to rub shoulders who would otherwise never have occasion to meet), Augurelli, old Bulwer, Fuzuli, and the mysterious Burnacs, whose extremely rare *Pièces détachées*, in a fine morocco binding with rounded corners, was aggressively displayed on a luxurious ebony bookstand.

I also remembered the smile that appeared on my friend's face the previous summer, when my eyes rested on a heavy, dark red volume lying on a low stool over which I had just stumbled for the third time.

'Look out! You seem to have something against my *Mizan al-huruf*!'

Seeing my stunned look, for despite all his knowledge, Flauzac's mouth did not adapt well to the requirements of pronouncing Arabic (in fact, I had heard something halfway between *missing ol' roof* and *Miss Anal Rough*), he added, more condescendingly than pedagogically, 'Come now, *Mizan al-huruf*, that is, *The Letter Scale*, by Jabir ibn Hayyan! It reveals all the secret characters . . . the ones sages have used since antiquity to give their ideas an enigmatic form.'

And he instantly grabbed the book and leafed through it, letting me glimpse, as he slowly turned the pages before my eyes, countless images: ideograms, symbols, and drawings, some of which struck me as genuinely beautiful.

When I cried out in surprise on seeing such strange figures associated with the names of Socrates, Plato, Aristotle, Pythagoras, Aesculapius, Hermes, and Polemon, he had, with decided magnanimity, taken the time to show me as well his copy of Jean Trithemius's *Steganography* (it was, naturally, the 1549 Lyons edition), thrusting under my nose the handful of pages (*famous* ones, he felt it necessary to add) devoted to the rules for substituting letters.

Obviously, I didn't pay much attention, at the time, to this

41

mass of details. But it was now clear that it was all this that was reemerging, with unaccustomed brutality, in the intuition that had just struck me. The book I held in my hands must belong to this set of more or less esoteric works.

But if so, why was it at my place?

Two hypotheses occurred to me.

Maybe Flauzac, wanting to initiate me to these mysteries, had surreptitiously slipped the book into the batch in order to help me discover a domain of which I was, in fact, quite ignorant? But that didn't seem much like him: he was not the kind of guy who is given to proselytizing old friends. And even if he were, he would certainly not have considered using indirect means for achieving his ends. On the contrary. He liked to say that he did not see friendship as a halfway kind of thing, and usually acted in the frankest, most direct way possible. So?

The other hypothesis, which was more plausible, was clearly right: It could only be a mistake. One of those terrible mix-ups all too frequent among people who also handle a great many books.

I knew that not long ago Flauzac had resumed his habit of working nonstop: he had even become the idol of several American journals (in particular, the one published at Fitchwinder University), which he provided with all sorts of scholarly contributions. He had also recently completed a number of translations (including Pu Songling's *Extraordinary Tales*), a study in comparative literature entitled 'From Jarry to Lowry,' and a long discussion of Roman allusions in the Tibetan epic. But above all, breaking with what had seemed to be for him an irreversible decision, he had been thinking about writing a book: A summa, for which he was accumulating, as was his habit, a copious body of documents. He spoke of it only guardedly. It concerned, I seemed to discern, various arcane sciences and was intended to take the form of a history of a peculiar struggle, a sort of long spiritual quest.

My wretched book must have gotten lost among a few dozen others that had piled up on the table after being hastily consulted in the excitement of one of those long work sessions from which you emerge in a sort of drunkenly exhausted state: your eyes burn, the first rays of dawn are like so many arrows shooting through the louvered shutters, and you're too tired to even think about tidying up before going in to collapse, fully clothed, on the bed, hardly taking the trouble to turn back the covers. When that happens, something that has been moved from its usual place is very likely never to return to it.

I already imagined my friend's frustration when, finding it necessary to locate a reference or check a quotation (a rather tedious task that he would have constantly put off, for weeks or even months, until he had arrived at a point when any further delay was impossible), he discovered, first with incredulity, and then with anger (since in addition the absence of any phantom would make the thing, in his view, inexplicable), that this volume, which he urgently needed at that very moment, and which he expected to be able to put his hands on immediately (for he remembered with the greatest precision the place to which he himself had assigned it), had mysteriously disappeared. I knew too well the state such a disappointment would put me in not to feel compassion for him; there's nothing worse than these untimely desertions, which elicit as much aggressiveness, suspicion, and jealousy as the worst infidelities, and from which I now try to protect myself by never letting anything leave my home.

But I immediately thought of the joy he would feel if, as I was now resolved to do, I returned his book to him the following day, accompanied by a short explanatory note, and also perhaps a few brief remarks – half-ironic, half-admiring – that reading it had inspired in me. Then everything would be okay again: the indispensable tool, diverted by mistake (but only for a short time, fortunately) from its function, would quickly resume its place, and Flauzac could once again consult it, in complete tranquillity.

To think that a moment earlier I was on the point of rejecting this book, angrily, aggressively, and even (why deny it?) with a certain scorn! The mistake was certainly one of my silliest blunders.

As a result of my initial doubt, I had committed a serious error. I urgently needed to back up.

SECOND MOVEMENT

Quarendo invenietis. – J. S. Bach

*Destroy all the world's libraries, keep only
a single volume, choose it at random,
and this volume will be the masterpiece
of the human intellect.*
– L. S. Mercier

4

And so I returned to the book with new ardor, and looked upon it with new eyes.

Scarcely had I taken it in my hands before it opened, by itself, to the first page that had caused my frustration. And my eyes, in a single movement, ran over the whole page.

Come on, dump this book. Or better yet, throw it as far away as you can. Right now. Before it's too late. That resolution is your only escape, believe me.

Now look up. Let your weary eyes rest on the peace of infinite horizons, large spaces punctuated only by trees, rocks, and clouds. Look away from these perverse lines.

What do you expect from them? What can you expect?

If you think you're going to meet a bosom buddy, a new friend with whom you can have one of those intimate conversations you've been dreaming about for such a long time, forget it. Go find someone else to listen to you and console you.

Or maybe you hope that by some miracle you're going to see your own image reflected here, more or less, or that you're suddenly going to recognize a little bit of your own thought. Maybe you even imagine (who knows how far your naïveté will go?) that you're going to find a guaranteed way of recovering the use of your own voice.

Or then again, at the last minute, you've convinced yourself (for you have gradually acquired a taste for certainties!) that things won't begin until you arrive, that you are the indispensable witness without whom nothing that happens here will have any meaning. And you expect to receive your reward for the gift you are going to make.

Unless your only concern is to dispel a moment of boredom, and your only goal is to go as far as you can into foreign territory, to discover worlds you've never seen before, to experience the pleasures and pains you've never had the courage to give to those around you.

Who cares what you expect, anyway? Whatever it is, you're going to be disappointed.

You have nothing in common, believe me, with the shades that are about to dance before your eyes. Their fate was sealed long ago, whereas you are still wondering what you're going to do at the next moment.

So why continue?

Well, you asked for it.

This book, which you have just entered rashly and without precautions, you still don't know that, like me, you may get lost in it.

I read this page, and then I reread it.

With all the pleasure I took from being certain, in advance, that I would find each word in the exact place where I knew that it was waiting for me, quietly, faithfully. Also with the firm conviction, long established in me because it had been inculcated by years of assiduous practice, at every stage of an unduly prolonged education, of the sacrosanct exercise of 'text explication' (which I am not about to give up), that to reread is always to read better.

However, like the precious gems whose appearance alters, people say, with the time and the season, the text had changed.

In-con-tes-ta-bly, as Flauzac liked to say.

It no longer elicited that feeling of repulsion that had struck me so strongly only a few minutes earlier. On the contrary, what was now dominant was interest. Or rather, the excitement arising from intense curiosity. But an excitement immediately tempered by a certain anxiety: how was I going to proceed in order to take possession of what had just offered itself to me?

I felt myself breathing more rapidly, and a slight flush spread over my face. I was as nervous as a boy going to his first tryst. And even a little more. A tryst presupposes a certain complicity, and at least minimal progress toward a common goal. Whereas with my text I was still in the preliminary stages.

I suddenly felt as though I were reliving certain moments (not necessarily the least disagreeable, as I remember them) of my adolescence.

Thus I found myself confronted by what I still called, with a slight tremor in my voice, *girls*. They intimidated me. I was particularly afraid of their shrill laughter when they gathered, in groups of three or four, when school was out, on the big square in front of the lycée, or on Saturday nights, for long, ritualistic perambulations down the main street of our remote suburb.

At that time, I did not like (and still do not like) to have to take the first step, the step that is rightly said to be the hardest but the one that makes everything else possible. Or rather, to be perfectly frank, I didn't know how. I was always afraid of going too far or not far enough. I began to feel at ease only when we had reached the stage of writing love letters: that stage, at least, caused me no problems, for one day I had swiped, without remorse, from a friend's library (he didn't even know, the wretch, that he possessed such a treasure), everything I needed to conduct all my amorous correspondence for years to come.

Thus I awaited, my heart in my throat, until the girl I had chosen (in general, after exchanging a few glances, as discreet as possible, in the propitious hubbub of our miniscule schoolyard, right under the noses of our teachers, or in the back room of the overheated café where we usually went) decided to approach me.

49

My whole amorous strategy (a strategy that is never so effective as in the hands of those who, preoccupied with conquest, know how to avoid falling in love) was long ago summed up in one of Laforgue's couplets, found by chance in one of the anthologies of which I was so fond:

Oh, if only, one fine evening, She would sigh,
And come on her own to drink at my lips, or die!

I repeated these magic lines to myself silently (but with a fervor almost as great as that I still brought, a few months earlier, to reading my daily prayers), while at the same time watching out of the corners of my eyes my future lover's movements toward me, sometimes full of promising resolution, sometimes more circumspect or even clearly hesitant. And the strangest thing is that it worked. To be sure, the recipe was far from infallible, and the success of my mute incantation was not absolutely guaranteed. But it's a fact that, to my great satisfaction, the miracle sometimes happened. And more than one girl came on her own volition, knowing instinctively, perhaps, that my gratitude for this spontaneous offering would be limitless.

Thus I let my attention hover for a moment, let my eyes drift, slide, zigzag over the surface of the text like a skater on the ice. But unlike a skater (who sees the water under his feet and tries not to fall into it), I did everything I could, on the contrary, to break the ice. Hoping that a word, an expression, would jump out and help me solve the little mystery that was preoccupying me. Who knew? Maybe I was going to be as lucky as Leonardo, who one day discerned, in the cracks of a decrepit wall, the precise outlines of a picture.

That is more or less what happened. Very quickly. Two words, among the first ones in the text, literally jumped out at me, forcing themselves on my attention with an unaccustomed power.

They were, naturally, the haughty imperatives that in fact constituted the content of the page as a whole.

Dump, throw, the text said. These two verbs of similar meaning could not have been juxtaposed by mere chance: why should the author have written 'throw' when 'dump' already said, and more vigorously, what needed to be said? In my view, it was clear that this little word 'throw,' with its five letters, was more than a simple (and in this case, superfluous) repetition: it transmitted a message!

The message was clear enough; all I had to do was read the word backwards (taking the combination *th* as a single unit, as in the Old English *thorn*), and *throw* became *worth*. This was almost too easy. Moreover, inverting the order of the letters also inverted the message conveyed by the word: rather than something valueless that should be thrown away, it told me, the book was a pearl of great worth!

The other word, *dump*, was more difficult to decipher, but in its privileged position at the beginning of the text, it was obviously of at least equal importance. Reading it backwards led nowhere; in fact, no anagrammatic permutation of its letters produced anything significant. Then it finally dawned on me: what I had to do was not rearrange but substitute. If I converted the final, unvoiced labial *p* into a voiced labial *b*, I got *dumb*. At first, I was tempted to see this as a negative commentary on the book, or on its reader, but the process involved in deciphering it gave me the clue I needed: it was a matter of *voicing* the consonant; the word meant, not 'lacking in intelligence,' but 'mute.' This was paradoxically confirmed by the fact that the *b* in the word 'dumb' is mute, as if reflecting the meaning of the word. But what could this mean? Only that the text was dumb, that it kept its secret, until it was made to speak. Thus the first word of the book, far from prohibiting me from reading the book, was actually inviting me to decipher it, to give it voice.

All this seemed to me to prove that there was something hidden in this text, a silent mystery, which I had to uncover, and that this mystery involved something of great worth. In a few moments I had already acquired, if not the key to the mystery, at least some important clues. All I had to do was continue.

Unfortunately, once I had taken this first step, the text closed up again. It refused to yield anything more. Slyly, it seemed to leave me to pursue, all by myself, the task of reading and making sense of what was passing before my eyes.

I therefore immediately set to work.

But I immediately confronted a problem: how was I to determine, on the basis of the supposedly coded message, the corresponding clear message, when I obviously knew nothing about the process of decoding? I was going to have to engage in a genuine effort of decipherment. This task did not intimidate me, because once again, the memory of certain things I'd read came to my rescue.

In fact, this kind of puzzle had fascinated me all through one part of my childhood – a part to which I still felt very close and which I was always ready to relive. I had read so many of those novels (without ever growing tired of them) in which we see the owner of a treasure, who is prevented by a terrible mischance from enjoying his possession (as if treasures were never to benefit those who took the trouble to amass and preserve them, but only the courageous or clever people who were able to brave all sorts of perils to find them at the other end of the world), doing his utmost to leave behind clues that will provide the point of departure for tracking it down!

The rule seems obvious, then, and can be reduced to a few cases that, following my predilection for logical classifications, I had long since inventoried.

Or else (and this is clearly very elementary) the writer and receiver of a secret message have previously agreed to use a code, and the addressee has only to refer to it. This code does not necessarily require, like Scott's, Count Gronsfeld's, or Lord Bacon's, a great amount of ingenuity. It can be very simple, like the one (the first that occurs to me) known as 'broken prose': to discover the true meaning of the message, one merely folds in half the sheet of paper it is written on, hiding half of it.

But there are, of course, far more complex codes. I had discovered one by accident. It had been created by the genius of the Abbé Trithemius, who was apparently cherished by my friend Flauzac, and whose name Sophie had one day mentioned, to my great surprise, with approval. Thanks to a system of equivalences, it used to permit lovers to exchange, in the guise of the most devout prayers, the most passionate declarations. Thus *I love you* was transformed into *Noble Venus, graceful star, genius is reborn in your soul.*

It goes without saying that none of these examples had anything to do with the text with which I was concerned.

The second case, which was closer to my own situation, is that in which the code, without having been the subject of an explicit agreement, is based on regular substitutions that the addressee can attempt, by trial and error, to locate and identify: as if there were, underlying all human words, a secret language in which everyone can, by making an effort, make himself understood.

Now, I had recently heard a bit of news on this subject that had greatly interested me. A distinguished essayist (a literary historian and a noted lexicographer to boot) had just demonstrated, in a way that had been found convincing by a group of connoisseurs, that some of the most admired pages in French literature were in fact the result of manipulations of this kind! They had been obtained by replacing, in an original version that remained mere babble, certain words (sometimes nouns, sometimes verbs,

53

sometimes both) by others that follow them, seven entries later, in a given dictionary. Thus the first sentence of *Madame Bovary*, which has become so famous that it seems to have flowed spontaneously from Flaubert's pen, was supposed to have had its source in this first, mysterious version: *Nous étions à l'étrille quand la Providence entra* (*We were using the currycomb when Providence entered*).

I could not resist the temptation to see if my text had undergone a similar treatment. I seized the closest dictionary and opened it. It took me only a short time to discover that had this system been used, the first words might have been, in their initial version, something like this: 'Comfort, dun this book. Or better yet, thrum away.' These three new verbs seemed to me to correspond rather well to the situation. To simultaneously comfort, that is, aid and abet, is just what the initial sentence of the ultimate version – when properly read – had urged me to do, and not once, but repeatedly, as if dunning the book to yield up its wealth. Thrumming, of course, suggested that I should play the book as if it were a musical instrument, striking chord after chord from it.

However, when I thought about it, this didn't seem to me wholly convincing. For the other substitutions, which I proceeded to make immediately afterward, were far less eloquent. And above all, there subsisted, so far as I was concerned, two great uncertainties. First of all, the choice of the dictionary: in the absence of any indication, how was I to know for sure which one was intended to be used as a reference? Among the countless dictionaries produced by specialized publishers, even if I limited myself to the three or four largest, the range of possibilities was extensive. Moreover, there was another question, no less troublesome: what distance was supposed to separate, in this dictionary, the masked word and the one that served as its substitute? I had opted for a distance of seven words, in conformity with the model I had heard mentioned. But nothing proved that this was the right choice. The only number that appeared explicitly in my initial text (through a reference, which had at first seemed to me highly arbitrary, to a parable from the Gospels), was eleven. This number, duly manipulated by me, led nowhere . . .

There remained the third hypothesis, in which the circumstances prevent any agreement, either explicit or implicit, between the sender and the receiver. In this case, the former always finds a way to deliver to the latter, in the body of the message itself, like the hidden signatures that nature is fond of putting on its creations, the key that will make decoding possible. This usually consists in a small inexactitude, a tiny deviation from normal usage, that can easily be overlooked by ordinary readers. A common word whose spelling has been purposely altered, an imperceptibly clumsy construction, a slightly shifted spacing, a few misplaced apostrophes, a few omitted commas in strategic locations, suffice to attract, like flashing red lights, the receiver's attention, to put a bug in his ear and allow him to reconstitute, little by little and with an ease we cannot help but admire, the whole code.

Feeling that I had discovered an infallible method (for I had never seen any of my favorite heroes stopped dead at the start of his adventures by a mere coded message), I set out in search of what was to become my Ariadne's thread. For this task I donned the spectacles of the most vigilant, most scrupulous proofreader. No anomaly, no matter how small, would escape me. I was resolved to spot anything that resembled a variance in the system of signs, to read every deviation as a meaningful trap. Prepared, in short, to scrutinize this page as I did, on some cold mornings (what upsetting or trivial secret did I hope, after all, to discover there?), the features of a face too much beloved.

The project began under the best auspices: the page that lay before my eyes contained a large number of peculiarities, and in any case far more than I had noticed during my initial reading, blinded as I was then by the fit of rage that had overcome me.

First of all, certain words seemed far darker than others. Was this an attempt to draw my attention to them, to force me to take them into account without delay? Or did it result instead from the use of a poor quality of ink? Hard to decide. For immediately afterward, it was the punctuation that intrigued me. It seemed to obey no precise rule. The greatest uncertainty was evident in the use of the comma and the period. And also, of course, in the use of colons: they all appeared and disappeared with a delightful capriciousness.

This second approach seemed to me the more promising. If I relied on the models I had in mind, the essence of the message ought to be found in the words that followed these erroneous or abusive punctuations. Unless it was in those that preceded them. The connection, in any case, was clear, and easy to test.

I quickly located other 'suspect' words: *book, escape, console, voice, sealed.* They were certainly neither the least important nor the least suggestive words in the text, and it was easy to imagine an itinerary on which they would be the chief stops, or which they would at least mark out. However, when I put them end to end, they did not seem to me to constitute a genuine message.

Although I combined them in every possible way, even going so far as to supply grammatical connectives that might clarify the meaning, I couldn't make anything out of them. At most, a few, isolated into groups of two, looked as though they might reward research ('sealed book') or indicate the methods to be used in understanding them ('escape substitutions,' 'voice console'). But it was all pretty vague and left me very unsatisfied.

To the point that I quickly began to doubt that I'd chosen the right path. Perhaps there was, in this typographical disorder through which hidden signals seemed so likely to be conveyed, nothing deliberate, nothing that couldn't be explained, in the most ordinary way, by the carelessness of the proofreader or printer.

I didn't want to lay too much importance on this disappointment. It was unanticipated, to be sure. But after all, in such matters you don't always succeed on the first try. Even in the best novels, you usually have to pass more than one test before you arrive at the goal.

If the clues I was looking for were not to be found in the programmed irregularities of orthography or typography, that was no doubt because they were hidden elsewhere. Thus it was no longer a matter of just reading, but of searching under the words themselves, as in a palimpsest, a meaning that their apparent form dissimulated: the message must be inscribed beneath!

My deduction seemed to me impeccable.

Therefore I threw myself joyfully into this new approach, whose difficulties I neither suspected nor gauged.

This involved a great deal, in truth, because it required me to read this page, which seemed composed of simple words, as a sophisticated assemblage of tiny enigmas. Rigor was required. And a sagacity equaling at least that of the venerable medieval commentators. Now, they really knew how to take apart every sentence, to tease out, with as much subtlety as boldness, the words concealed beneath the words. Charades, rebuses, anagrams, chronograms, and all the marvelous constructions that lent themselves so well to disguises – the medieval commentators overcame them all. They knew all the ways of detecting countless routes through the heart of the most hermetic utterance. Their minds had long since become used to this kind of labor.

Mine wasn't sufficiently used to it.

Nevertheless, I tried to reconstitute at least some of the numberless designs potentially woven into the words: simple or complex geometrical figures (crosses, diamonds, circles), and even the floor plans of certain buildings: a cathedral with its bays and chapels, a chateau surrounded by all its defenses.

To that end, I found it necessary to begin by completely rewriting my text. An absurd task, some will say, those for whom writing has remained the 'dummy's knowledge' mocked in the upper level of my elementary school. However, I immediately set to work with a joy I could hardly contain. This was because I was borne along in my labors by a whole retinue of precious memories: my first wooden pencil box, its scaly varnish covered with spots; in a little metal case, my assortment of writing implements, each adapted to a different kind of writing, jealously protected like a treasure; my collection of blotters permeated with an odor that I made no attempt to identify, at the time, but which I learned, much later, was that of chicory; finally, the white porcelain inkwell, always brimming with the violet ink that, under my mother's anxious eyes (she feared, not without reason, the damage my clumsy haste made almost inevitable), I made myself, using a strange powder, particularly soiling, bought in a tiny shop with a very high ceiling, in which a little old man with a corkscrew beard officiated, perched atop a teetering metal stool.

It is true that a person who copies has only to close his eyes in order to glimpse, looking over his shoulder, a glorious lineage of tutelary shades. There is a kind of magic in manipulating the pen or the calamus, a sweet, drunken exhilaration. What do we know

58

about a text whose letters we have not ourselves shaped, one after the other, with their loops, downstrokes, and upstrokes? Is there any better way to make it our own (an operation that requires slow, careful work) than to repeat by ourselves the whole extent of its itinerary, sentence after sentence, page after page? It is not long before the scribe's alleged humility gives way to the proprietor's pride.

My text once copied, I immediately had to change its arrangement, to transform it into a gigantic magic square, in which the combinations of letters could be read in every direction. I spent a long time laboriously counting and recounting the characters and calculating the precise dimensions of the future square.

It proved impossible to arrive at any genuine result. All I was able to obtain, not without difficulty and after several fruitless attempts (for I quickly got lost in my calculations), was the discovery that the words in the text seemed to number 349 (*three hundred forty-nine*). But although this number was certainly not fortuitous, it was unclear to me just what I could do with it.

Perhaps Flauzac might have been able to suggest a solution. But there was no way I was going to bother him for that! I would have liked to be able, all by myself, to discover some elegant numerical arrangement in the text, to discern the resonances and harmonies that flowed from it, and to savor all the pleasure this normally gives connoisseurs!

Alas, the realm of numbers is not one in which I feel at ease: Unlike Flauzac, who saw numbers as *marvelous, delicious friends* and had soon learned how to tame them, I had always seen them as dangerous. This had begun very early on, during my first two years of elementary school: My memory stubbornly refused to register any kind of calculation; so that on some winter mornings, the fear of having to undergo questioning on the multiplication table was enough to unleash in my organism strange disorders that kept me, writhing with pain (which was genuine, whatever my family may have thought), in my bed. And I never had the occasion, afterward, to set that unfortunate situation right.

In the course of this new stage in my research, I had not advanced one iota. This left me both disappointed and irritated.

'But isn't that,' I said to myself to calm my impatience, 'what happens with every truly innovative text?'

That was a meager consolation, and pretty artificial to boot! It didn't keep me from feeling tired, just enough to spend a few moments stretched out on my couch while waiting for new inspirations to strike me.

The certainty of Sophie's impending arrival soon perked up my spirits.

It seemed clear that I was going to have to change my strategy. Immediately retreat to a kind of research better suited to my abilities. More like the sort of thing purveyors of oracles do. Now, what has all the authority of sibyls, necromancers, prophets, pythonesses, oneiromancers, and fortune-tellers been based on, for centuries, if not the more or less obscure use of words with double meanings and equivocal formulas? To the point that the history of divination (and who knows, maybe History itself, despite its great age) might, without doing much harm to anyone (on the contrary), be reduced to a vast collection of puerile approximations and puns that anyone could justifiably consider detestable.

Therefore, it was with renewed confidence that I undertook to track down everything in my text that resembled an ambiguity or amphibology. Here I was, fortunately, on familiar ground. I had long been convinced that a word always contained much more than just itself: there was no word, even the most innocent-looking, that, bearing multiple, divergent, contradictory meanings, was not likely to be playing a double or triple game. From a new angle, more conscious and more systematic this time, I more or less returned to my first intuition, to the inaugural signal transmitted by the words *dump* and *throw*.

I was immediately halted by the word *resolution*: wasn't it obviously this word that must contain the solution? It was fairly bulging with different trails to be followed, and not only because of its strong, lingering odor of alchemy! However, I had to disregard it; its usage here, in the sense of a *firm decision made after mature consideration*, seemed clear enough.

I tried to continue, but I could get no further; my eyes, which were used to locating the allusion beyond the letter, now looked through the text as the sun passes through a windowpane. No, I couldn't see anything, not a single one of those misleading words that the reader suddenly discovers (always too late, unfortunately for him) that he initially misunderstood. My author was obviously no more an adept of this ancient form of disordering the senses than I was.

5

It occurred to me that a little music might calm my nerves, and help me overcome my disappointment. It might even be able to absorb my preoccupations, as it had been able to absorb, in the worst moments of my past life, so many things.

So I turned on the radio. I immediately recognized the first measures of the *Wanderer Fantasy*, in an old recording (with Alfred Brendel) that was also part of my own collection. This was, in my system of interpretation (a highly complex model I had perfected after years of meticulously observing all those encounters that are often rather hastily assumed to be products of mere chance or coincidence), an ambiguous sign. I tried to see only its positive side. For me, this recording had a strong affective charge: it had been given me by my mother and had always been one of my favorites.

Deeply absorbed in the music, I did not hear the telephone ring. Or rather I heard it, but (as often happens to me) too late: the caller hung up just as I picked up the receiver.

This incident annoyed me. Not that I have any particular delight in telephone conversations. I've never been able to get away from untimely calls, undesirable callers, unduly prolonged conversations. But that day was a special day. I was expecting only one call – Sophie's – that could make or break the rest of my life. And now, because I had been momentarily unavailable, my attention having been stupidly focused on something else, I might have just missed it.

There was no doubt that she would be surprised by my failure to answer the phone. She knew my homebody habits, of which she disapproved, but which she in fact tolerated well enough.

The preceding day, I had reminded her of my birthday, and I had assured her that I wouldn't budge from my place until she arrived; I had even asked her, with an emphasis that must have seemed to her excessive, to come *at any hour of the day or night*.

So I was furious with myself. I was afraid that this incident might result in a misunderstanding. One of those misunderstandings that were becoming increasingly common between us: apparently trivial at the beginning, but leading in the long run to serious disappointments, they were undermining, with alarming speed, the lovely harmony with which our relationship had started.

On the third day, at dawn, while I was innocently dreaming up plans for our future life together (for I already considered this common future as an established fact), she had said to me, ironically humming the 'Prends garde à toi' from *Carmen*, that she would not tolerate any restriction of her freedom. Thus it was agreed that she alone would decide when we met, how often, and how long our affair would last, and that I was not even to try to write to her or call her. Then I understood that she lived, except for the few moments she was prepared to devote to me, in a distant world to which she did not wish, for reasons only she knew, to give me access. I imagined with rage a brilliant society, spectacular departures at dusk, wild gallops in the early morning hours, packs of lovers . . .

The exhilaration of the first days, which I had been vain enough to believe she shared (at the time, she did nothing to deprive me of my illusion), seemed to be evaporating. To my ecstasies Sophie now responded only with a restraint that troubled and worried me. Our meetings became increasingly rare, sometimes almost fleeting, as if her excessively perfect body were one of those that could not long endure being possessed. And I came away exhausted, these too brief instants of fusion leaving me still more alone.

But perhaps the worst thing was that I had the impression, which was accentuated every time we met, that she distrusted me. She began to say very little, never replying to any of my questions. Or if I did succeed in drawing her into conversation, she hastened, more attentive to the words I pronounced than to the content of what I was saying, to seize the possibilities of escape or diversion that language always provides. When sometimes it was she who took the initiative in an exchange, I was never sure I really understood the sentences she uttered: coming from her mouth, words had a different meaning, a different resonance, and the weight of what she had to say seemed far too great to be entrusted to ordinary language.

Even in our embraces, she didn't give me much of herself. Not even the harmless trivialities any random woman met in a bar after midnight gives you without charge. In particular, she did not indulge in the nocturnal murmuring, the pillow talk, full of mad laughter, plans, and confessions, that I believed to be an indispensable to the life of a couple. Loving, talking, talking, expressing oneself, and seducing in that very way – these had been, for me, consubstantial activities.

Perhaps, I thought, *she found that initial happiness, in which I had so quickly established myself, too vulgar to be appropriate for the marginal being she was.* I came, quite naturally, to wonder whether she didn't regret this whole adventure, whether she was thinking about breaking, as soon as possible, a bond that already oppressed her.

Nevertheless, I persisted. For it now seemed to me impossible to get along without her. To be sure, there is a long list of couples who have loved only at a distance and separated from each other: I had no desire for us to be one of them! I needed Sophie, her eyes on me, her outlook on the world. I needed every pore of her skin. I needed her hands, which sometimes seemed to live an autonomous life. It had become, on my part, a constant, tormented, impatient pursuit. As if Sophie were now entrusted with all the secrets, the only person capable of answering my questions.

Weeks went by, and I saw clearly that everything was going to fall apart. But what could I do? What could I do? Of those first, miraculous moments, when I had stupidly believed I possessed her completely and forever, soon all that remained to me was ashes. On some days I felt a curtain of tears about to fall over my eyes.

However, I tried to console myself, on those days, by clinging to a few ancient illusions. I pretended to believe that my suffering was not in vain: I was undergoing a series of tests; they would ineluctably lead me toward the happy denouement which, from all eternity, was due me.

The approach of summer finally gave me an idea.

I proposed a trip. To Greece, for example, or along the Ionian coast. I hoped that an escape to the places where she had lived for a long time in her youth (this was one of the few details about her life that she had spontaneously vouchsafed me), and for which she retained a fondness mixed with nostalgia (for there, I thought I understood, she had been loved by some eminent men, and with a love at least equal to my own), would bring us together, help us to rediscover our ephemeral golden age. Perhaps I would also finally succeed in finding the time, which I had always lacked, to get to know her and to make myself known to her.

Thus, letting myself dream (and this is surely the one of my faculties that I have most fully developed, to the point that I would be prepared, on some days, to count among the great achievements of my life certain actions carried out during my sleep), I imagined a pilgrimage punctuated by the wildest gambols. And I described it to her, when she consented to listen to me.

Together, under the warm, late-afternoon sun, in one of those Ionian islands still unknown to travelers, we would go to commune with each other under the nearly intact columns of a temple that no guide had pointed out for centuries. To get there, we would have to take, laughing with delight, impossible goat-paths. We would not hesitate to climb up and then descend the slippery tiles, jumping across ancient ditches full of brambles. Just before nightfall, we would return along those narrow paths where you never meet anyone, except perhaps peasants dressed in black leading donkeys loaded with olive branches. Sometimes we would stop briefly, when a nest of hay or leaves offered us its hospitality, to rest a moment. A lovely moment, under the stars. And, while the birds, high above, traced large circles, and the spectacle of the sky and the stars gradually appeared with its accustomed majesty, I would watch over her sleeping body, running my fingers lightly over the rounded slope of her thighs, or caressing the curve of her nearly naked breasts.

She let me talk, smiling with an absent air at my passionate speeches. But I was only too aware of what her silence meant: She was making fun, and cruelly, of what she had one day called the *ancient poetic dreams of an adolescent from another era*. And I finally sheepishly recognized that this whole phantasmagoria was in fact puerile.

Of course, I had to give up on Greece, and even on any idea of a trip with her. As if all that had suddenly become something inconceivable. In exchange, I obtained what I took to be a concession on her part: Sophie promised to do her best to make her visits more regular, and less brief. A promise that, despite my insistent reminders, she hardly kept.

Therefore I had counted very heavily on this evening. And the idea that, through my own fault, the visit I had so much sought might be compromised only increased my fury.

But what could I do? There was no solution except to wait for another call, hoping it wouldn't be too long in coming. Sophie knew very well that I never stayed away from home for any length of time.

Night had fallen. Long ago, no doubt. A very clear night, after the storm (I had scarcely heard it, despite its violence) that had swept the clouds from the sky.

Mechanically, I picked up my book again.

I turned on a light, rediscovering with pleasure the vaguely oriental reflections given the room by the Indian lampshade (a gift from Marc, on the occasion of my moving in). Very quickly, I felt my anger dying down. The silence of the night began to have its beneficial effect. No matter what troubles I have with sleep, I have always had a special relationship with darkness, with night. As if the assurance of having a long period of immobility and stability, after daylight has disappeared, sufficed to change my relationship to things.

As a child, I discovered very early on another reason for loving the long holiday meals at home, punctuated with songs, laughter, and prayers: their length allowed me to go to bed far past my usual bedtime. On those evenings, I was no sooner in bed than instead of falling asleep, I became doubly attentive, struggling with all my power to remain awake in order to listen, as long as I could, to the tick-tock of the big grandfather clock in the living room. Its regular rhythm, which seemed inexhaustible, fascinated me. I intensely wanted, at least once, to experience the magical moment when everything flips over, when one passes from today to tomorrow, or rather from yesterday to today. For I refused to believe that an operation of such importance (*To do that, you have to move heaven and earth*, one of my uncles, a sometime poet, used to say) could take place without some dark splendor, and I wanted to be associated with the ceremonial that my imagination had patiently elaborated for the occasion.

Even now, after the always somewhat disturbing stage of twilight, darkness acts on me like a drug: nothing like it for helping my thought take flight far from the powers that usually hold it captive, or for helping it, on the contrary, to descend deeper and deeper into unexplored zones that it forces, pitilessly, to reveal themselves. Thus, persuaded that knowledge is acquired at night, at those moments when words suddenly seem heavy with additional light, with greater brilliance, I have never doubted the fecundity of staying up late. Indeed, a single lamp burning all by itself in the middle of the night gives me a feeling of power: everything seems within my grasp.

No question, then, of wasting such a moment in *complacent nostalgia, sentimental soppiness* (Sophie's way of talking had begun to permeate, without my knowing it, my own private language). The fever, the ferment, were too strong: I was sure that the mechanism, once set in motion again, would be able to run by itself.

And then, the failure of my efforts (which seemed to me obvious) could only be temporary. In the course of history, people have managed to decipher texts much more difficult than this little page by a perverted pseudocryptographer, who was, moreover, provincial and pretentious. Completely unknown alphabets, languages that had long remained mysterious, had eventually yielded up their secrets. Scholars like Tyschen, Münter, and Grotefend had attacked Assyro-Chaldean and triumphed over it. Not to mention, of course, giants like Champollion and Ventris. It is true that the latter had character, method, quite a bit of luck, and logical minds: at the age of ten, Champollion had already acquired a facsimile of the Rosetta Stone, and Ventris was fourteen when he heard Sir Arthur Evans lecture on Linear B and thus discovered the existence of the mysterious Aegean writing that he was later to . . . etc.

So I was sure that this page, no matter how tough it seemed, would finally reveal its secret. The hope of soon succeeding kept me mentally alert. When you know how to ask questions, the answers are always there, everywhere, always: islands of clarity emerge from the fog, but so suddenly that you are at first afraid you haven't really seen them.

Just one problem: how to find the right angle of approach, which the author had maliciously concealed. He must have had a good laugh thinking about the difficulties anyone who tried to decipher this very limpid page was going to have. But he had responded in advance to all sorts of curious questions, in a form whose perfect logic, whose placid transparency, appeared only a posteriori, when the first elements of the barrier had fallen. Then everything would come all at once.

New hypotheses began to emerge, in great numbers.

First, I thought of the ancient procedure of the acrostic, so prized, along with the other techniques of *notariqon*, by my beloved Kabbalists (and precisely by the great Abulafia, the first I had encountered). They made dizzying use of it, and their virtuosity allowed them to discover, in certain passages of Genesis that in no way attracted my attention a priori (except, perhaps – and this was unexpected at the heart of a text supposed to have been written by God Himself – a dose of the prosaic and the banal that was, frankly, excessive), marvelous hidden meanings.

I immediately set to work. With enthusiasm, but also with a certain circumspection: it seemed to me that I was about to undertake the ascent of an unknown peak. Equipped with the thickest of my felt pens, I proceeded to line up, on big white sheets of paper, in fat capital letters, the first letters of the first words in the text, which yielded more or less the following:

CODTBOBYTIAFAAYCRNBITLTRIYOEBM

then the first letters of the sentences:

CORBTNLLWWIGOMOAUWWYTS

and even, just to be sure, the first letters of the paragraphs:

CNWIOOUWYSWT

each time expecting to see emerge, reconstituted letter by letter, the message finally unveiled.

It didn't happen. These letters, no matter how they were arranged, didn't reveal anything. To my great confusion. In what I had taken pleasure in thinking of as an ascent, I had apparently missed the first step.

So then I left the initial letters alone in order to examine the order of the words. First I tried the palindrome, reading my text backward:

it in lost getting of risk the running you're me like that know don't still you precautions without and rashly entered just have you which book this.

The cacophony of the result was immediately evident. To the point that I didn't even feel the need to pursue the experiment further, for instance, by exploring the possibility of a palindrome that involved not the letters or the words, but the meanings.

Once again, I had to look elsewhere.

Why not try, for example, arranging the words, or groups of words, in new combinations? Not hesitating to push the exercise to its most extreme limits, I systematically tested all the possible permutations. First of all, the nouns: on the model of rhymes, I performed permutations into couplets, cross-rhymes, rhymes in envelope form. Then I turned to the adjectives and verbs, which

71

I subjected to the same manipulations. Is it necessary to describe here the mediocre result of all this work? You can guess it easily enough. It can be reduced to two words: incoherence and absurdity.

The text, in its stubbornness, rejected my approaches, and I found this resistance taunting. Was I going to give up? By accepting, for example, the convenience of assuming that the nonsense was intentional? After all, some of the directions I had up to that point rejected with disdain could offer me an acceptable recourse, an honorable way out.

Yes, but something was still bothering me. Nothing proved that the key I was looking for had to be a simple key, that it involved a single coding system. It could be multiple, complex: every paragraph, every line, even every word or group of words might very well be part of a different system . . .

I began to feel poorly equipped for my task: I had confidently cast all the nets at my disposal, and had caught nothing other than shapeless debris, hardly worthy of a genuine revelation.

However, I would have been satisfied with the most intangible reference! It would have sufficed to make me throw myself into the breach. Then I could have made massive use of the resources of exegesis and flushed out, without striking a blow, wherever it was hidden, the allegorical meaning, the moral meaning, the anagogic meaning. The whole history of humanity proves that metaphorical interpretation has infinite resources, and that there is no text that it cannot save.

Despair was not far off.

Everything now seemed to be happening as in one of those dreams in which, hastening to reach the opposite bank, you rush onto a bridge, only to discover, after a few steps, that you're up to your neck in water.

My last lance (or at least what I thought was my last lance) had just been broken. It was my own fault, of course: who else would have reduced this text to the level of a rebus, and then raised it to that of an enigma?

I had every reason to cut a sorry figure. Nonetheless, through a paradox I didn't even try to conceal from myself, my fascination was in no way diminished.

To be sure, I told myself, it was only one page, with all that word (whose sonorities I have always found sweet and seductive) implies in the way of the incomplete, separate, partial, and fragmentary: was it right to consider it in isolation, to ignore, deliberately, the environment within which it might take on its true meaning?

But an answer to my doubts had gradually suggested itself: what was now before my eyes was far more than a page of a book, it was a very singular object, conceived, as if purposely, to nourish my reverie or my meditation.

And above all, I couldn't get rid of this formula, which went round and round in my head like a stubborn refrain:
co-ded-thus-de-co-able-co-ded-thus-de-co-able-co-ded-thus-de-co-able . . .

There was, of course, another solution. An indirect solution.

It forced itself on me. With growing insistence.

Up to that point, I had tried to reject it, or at least to pretend to myself that I was not thinking about it (not seriously, anyway). But now I was obliged to consider it.

It was one of the simplest solutions, and I am prepared to wager that anyone but me would have resorted to it from the outset. It consisted in a single word, in a name: Flauzac. A simple phone call, and I would be relieved of my questions!

It was only a little past two in the morning. Flauzac rarely went to bed early, especially on Sundays. Thus I could, the very next minute, provided that he was home (but my friend, who had resumed in Bourges the habits of his youth, did not like to go out at night), learn the truth. And from the lips of the very one who, no doubt involuntarily (I did him this credit), was responsible for my difficulties. Know what to think of this strange work (of which I had not been able to decipher even the title!) and its enigmatic author. Know why it had turned up at my place and how I should behave with regard to it.

I picked up the phone and slowly dialed the number. But while I was doing it, something irresistible was making me see this act as a desertion: so once again, I was going to hasten to the aid of my adversary! When, after a short silence, the phone began to ring, more stridently than usual, at my friend's home, I slammed down the receiver.

My phone immediately began to ring, and this made me jump.

This time, Sophie didn't have to wait. She had hardly finished dialing my number before I answered. This put her in a good mood: like me, she adored such tiny coincidences. Our conversation was long, almost tender. At least, she had remembered my imminent fortieth birthday. But not to the point of wanting to come help celebrate it: when I asked her what time she thought she'd arrive, she answered, with a special quiver in her voice in which I detected a slight regret, that I'd better not expect her. And she immediately hung up.

I hadn't said anything to her about the book. Not a word concerning what I'd been doing all day. Why this omission, which I was well aware did not proceed from either chance or negligence? I myself didn't know. Was I beginning to mistrust her, too? I quickly rejected, with a certain embarrassment, that ridiculous idea. No, I believe it was rather a sort of reflex on my part. Like the kind of lies, usually concerning details that I considered negligible (the precise time when I got out of school, the name of the pal with whom I had lingered to play), that I sometimes took pleasure in telling my family when I was a child. These gave me the feeling that I finally had something I didn't owe to anyone else, something I had fabricated myself, that belonged to me alone: a secret. What a joy it was finally to be able to use, intentionally, this word that was so 'adult,' and to enjoy the slight torment that it produced! For an instant, this gave me a little bit of the self-assurance I lacked.

At that point, I noticed that I was hungry. It's true, I hadn't eaten anything since the enormous cup of tea and the dry biscuits (too dry) I'd had for breakfast.

I knew the refrigerator was empty. Nothing remained in the cupboards after the last cleanup Sophie had forced me to make. An expert in nutrition, among other things, she was very critical of what I ate, finding that the meager leftovers that always filled my old refrigerator played far too great a role in my diet; I spent hours combining them in creative mixtures that no one but me found appetizing (no doubt because they sometimes reminded me, when they succeeded, of my mother's cooking). In fact, she would have liked me to give up this practice (to which I was very attached) altogether, and to follow her example in eating only fresh foods.

I therefore had to fall back on the freezer; fortunately, Sophie had not yet had time to scrutinize its contents. I took out two packages, the last ones, tattered, hard, and white with frost, that had been in there for months. They were to constitute, on this memorable birthday Sunday, my only true meal: a fairly thick chateaubriand (which turned out to be tough) and a puff pastry (which turned out to be rather doughy). No fresh bread; I still had a few biscuits, whose vaguely sugary blandness nauseated me when I first bit into them, but which I stubbornly chewed up. Not having any wine, I opened a bottle of the German mineral water (Apollinaris was the brand, I think) whose effervescence I had liked ever since Flauzac had introduced me to it.

All this was quickly put away. Without the slightest pleasure, and not without melancholy. For that evening, had Sophie not failed to show up, I had dreamed of a quite different sort of festivities.

But at least my belly was more or less full.

I went back to my book, refusing, in spite of everything, to give up.

This time, my fatigue was too much for me. It was time for me to suspend the disorganized activity of my mind. Therefore I resigned myself to getting a little rest.

No, decidedly, I had already meditated too long on this page, reasoned too much about it. My bed, the ultimate refuge, was waiting for me.

6

When I drew back the covers on my bed, the whiteness of the sheets (changed that very morning) hurt my eyes. I tried to turn down the lamp, but leaning over it too quickly, I hit the bulb, which immediately burned out with a discreet sizzle. I did not think it necessary to replace it immediately (in reality, I didn't feel like climbing the stepladder to get, at the top of the only cupboard in the kitchen, a new bulb).

As on the preceding night, but for quite different reasons, I slept very badly; and, in the end, very little.

Of all the kinds of sleep I had experienced in recent months (these were very numerous, for during this troubled period, sleep had become a problem for me, and for that very reason, a constant object of observation), the one I endured that evening was distinguished by some unusual features.

At first, it was like hand-to-hand combat; hardly had I begun to fall asleep than I found myself struggling with a compact collection of indeterminate objects whose weight on my chest made me feel as if I were suffocating.

But immediately afterward, my sleep was disturbed by the intrusion of phantasmagoric figures. These in no way resembled the beings that peopled my childhood dreams. Neither ogres, nor werewolves, nor vampires, nor bogeymen. Not even the old demon with a hairy tongue riding a goat, whom I had eventually gotten used to because of his goat's good-humored air. These were made by piling up letters, of all sizes and fonts, compressed into strange pyramids: these unstable blocks, which sometimes seemed to be floating a few centimeters above the ground, were constantly collapsing, only to immediately reconstitute themselves and collapse again, never looking like anything more than a blackish mass of swarming centipedes. The letters, which were light, came together, then stretched out in long, dark rivers that silently flowed downhill. The words, when I managed nonetheless to see one or two as they passed by, were empty: like shells on a beach. Then I became a letter myself among the others, and ended up melting into this magma. And losing myself in it. No place for me in any of the groups that were forming. Hardly had I touched them when they collapsed, then disappeared into a sort of suddenly opening crevasse, ridiculously caulked with a few wads of crumpled paper.

This went on for a very long time, interrupted by short pauses during which, concerned, I wondered whether I was asleep or awake, whether I was dreaming or thinking.

Finally, however, I opened my eyes, not knowing exactly who I was or where I was. A ray of sunlight was hitting me right in the face. The apartment seemed to be swimming in a very unusual brilliance. I was drenched with sweat.

I was sure I'd slept for several days. It was not yet quite noon.

I spent no time trying to figure out what distant or profound realities were at work in the parade of images that had occupied my night. Standing before the mirror, shaving, I continued my dream, as if I had been granted the power to direct it as I wished.

And suddenly, it seemed to me that I saw things more clearly.

What had happened was that a new question had emerged, which was perhaps going to let me start over with a certain hope. Hadn't I simply, from the outset, taken the wrong path? No doubt in my haste as an apprentice in the trade of hermeneutics, and on the strength of various childish memories on which I had clearly relied excessively, I had misidentified the problem. It must be of a completely different nature than I had at first thought.

What was it all about, then? Tracking meaning down in its deepest lairs, right? Well . . .

Writing, of course, usually conveys messages. That is one of its chief vocations. Indeed, it is for that very purpose, some intelligent people say, that it was invented; but this is hotly contested by others who are just as intelligent (it's not for me to arbitrate this age-old quarrel). However, writing is not the only thing entrusted with this noble function! A tongue (I refer to that precious, fleshy organ, elongated, mobile, located in the mouth and used to taste, swallow, and speak) might have something to say about that. Here I came back to the allegedly dumb, that is to say, speechless, nature of my text, which I had discerned very early on, and too quickly forgotten.

I, too, had just fallen into the error of all those exegetes who, for far too long (and for texts far more important than this modest page) have chosen to neglect the oral, and reduced everything that was not written to a dependent, mediocre, subaltern position! Nonetheless, I was not unaware – without needing to refer to the writings of Bede Chang Cheng Ming on the *Cheu-King* or those of Van Bulck on eastern Bakongo – of the weight of the living word that issues from living lips.

Had I not heard it said a hundred times, in my childhood, that there are people for whom everything begins with the ear, and that the most important word in the first books of the Bible is the verb 'listen'? Had I not myself repeated, before the most diverse audiences (and even recently, in telling Sophie the story of my life), that all the great masters we revere, from Pythagoras to Socrates, from Buddha to Jesus (and I'm leaving some out), taught orally, and only orally?

Who knows, then, if the silent reading that, following a hoary custom in the West, I had practiced up to this point was not the obstacle that was preventing me from making further progress in understanding this page? It was urgent to reanimate all these words, to restore to the book its ancient (and almost congenital) complicity with the lips.

It was only too obvious that here lay the solution that had escaped me since the preceding day: by letting the syllables come out freely and meet each other, I was going to discover their hidden interaction; here, the oral would not merely repeat the written, but provide it (as among those peoples who, in saying their prayers, accord less importance to the sacred text than to the vibrations of the voice entrusted with performing the ritual recitation, or attribute to sounds, on the condition that they be properly modulated, the power to kill or give life) with indispensable complements. Who knows if the right voice, the appropriate intonation, were not going to produce miraculous metamorphoses?

And then, I have to admit that whatever my passion for books, I have a particular love for the arts of the voice. If I were ever to write the slightest page, my first concern would certainly not be to *publish* it (that is, to put it into circulation in the form of a cold, printed sheet of paper, among that mass of indifferent strangers called the public), but rather to read it myself, aloud, before a group of friends.

Declamation is an exercise to which I am bound by an old affection, associated with certain moments in my youth.

First of all, to the pleasure given me, despite my timidity, by the scholarly exercise (somewhat forgotten today) called *recitation*. Every week, the number of texts that I might be called upon to *recite* was increased by one or two: long series of classical alexandrines, with the intermediate caesura clearly marked. My memory, clinging to the rhymes and to the rhythm, drank in these verses without much effort, and once the first (inevitable) moments of stage fright had been overcome, I reproduced them without serious errors.

But my devotion also had less anecdotal justifications. The exercise of reading, perhaps the last vestige of a universe in which gesture and rhythm had full rights, has retained for me the aroma of very ancient things. Indeed, of that time (hardly imaginable today) when the world of letters was not yet a world of mute people wearing glasses. Then, a work met its first admirers in those moments of grace when, borne by the breath of the very person who had long worked secretly to fashion it, it issued, amid reverent contemplation, from a human mouth.

I am fond of the voice's power to abolish time at will, or at least to suspend its flight. Think of priests, no matter what religion they serve: they have only to pronounce the words prescribed by the ritual in order for the acts that the ritual commemorates to be repeated, identically, in a constantly renewed incarnation.

I like to be able to hold myself at attention to listen for the rise, after a long period of silence, and at the very time that (words having delicately slipped over the rough surface of the tongue) it is fusing with a new text, the voice that I do not immediately recognize as my own.

I like to imagine that when it comes out of my gullet, a text is spoken for the first time. Better yet: I know for sure that it is, at that moment, my creation.

So I went back to my page.

No doubt, to restore to the words their lightness, their original transparency, it would suffice to reread them out loud. Words, faithful to their ancient vocation as winged objects, would fly away. And thus I would rediscover the timbre, the intonations, that normally convey as much meaning as the body of the discourse itself, and whose absence is so often a source of misunderstandings. For only the voice can represent even the blanks in the text, those famous, apparently vacant spaces, in which we have long known (at least since an unforgettable page in the *Zohar*) that so many things (and some of the most essential) are expressed. It would restore to the whole that inner respiration through which the author's message would finally make itself heard, along with all the raillery and distress that I thought I could already divine in him.

I hazarded a few quick glances in order to be sure that there was no one around who might hear me: as a new tenant, I didn't want to spoil my reputation too soon and be taken for an eccentric (this description of me, meant as an insult, given at a meeting of co-owners in the back room of the City Hall bar and tobacco shop by the manager of a building who probably didn't know what it meant, had already caused me to lose my previous apartment). In order to avoid any risk, I would perhaps have to go hide in the basement somewhere. But in taking possession of my apartment, I had neglected to ask about the location of my part of the basement and had not thought about it since. So I limited myself to carefully closing the shutters on the two windows and hurried to shut myself up in my miniscule bathroom.

There, finally feeling safe, I went back to my book. It opened by itself to exactly the right page, and that again seemed to me a good omen.

Sitting on the edge of my claw-foot tub (which Sophie, who liked to take long baths in almost boiling water, found – rightly, I have to admit – very uncomfortable), facing the triple mirror in which my face, which was difficult to recognize, was only half reflected (sometimes in one of the mirrors, sometimes in another, and only intermittently), I once again immersed myself in the text. I wanted to let happen that sort of incubation through which the mind ends up molding itself to all the contours of what it is reading. But my position quickly proved both inconvenient and dangerous – I was constantly on the verge of slipping.

It was clearly wiser to simply get into the tub; at least I would have a backrest, and I could put my book on my knees if I raised them to the right height. Before getting into the empty basin fully dressed, I did take the precaution of quickly removing my shoes and socks; the cold sensation on the soles of my feet would help me stay awake.

Thus set up, I first made a few trials. I wanted to test the quality of the ambient air, its aptitude for reverberating in a suitable way the sounds I was about to emit.

Satisfied, I immediately began a genuine declamation. As theatrical and grandiloquent as one could wish. The voice strong and confident. Without a hesitation. Without a quiver. For I was beginning to know my page pretty well, and in all its articulations. Incontestably, it lent itself to certain effects. Ah, these injunctions, interjections, interrogations! And that amalgam of irony, pathos, and rhetoric. I was enjoying myself!

I passed every word through my mouth, without hurrying. Probing with delight their sonorous pulp, savoring the delicate balance of consonants and vowels, discovering at just the right point the sweet haven of the mute e's, I sought, in the initially harmonious melody of these sounds (which later, in a series of jerks, became voiceless), in their echoes, the traces, no matter how slight, of a signal (if need be, in the form of a dissonance or discordance) that would set my voice on the right path. As in those dreams whose meaning appeared to me (but then with what clarity!) only at the moment that I finished telling about them, it seemed to me that my throat, which held the solution without knowing it, was immediately going to reveal it to me.

But the effect on me was so unexpected that I wondered whether I hadn't made changes without realizing it.

To tell the truth, this almost always happens when I read aloud. No matter what the text (even a very familiar poem), no matter what the consequences (professional or even official), I have a hard time respecting the agreement (or rather the rigorous coincidence) that should in theory unite what is said with what is actually written on the page.

Thus the end of my declamation left me in a somewhat awkward position.

One thing seemed to me to have been established: the author had clearly retained, from somewhere in his past, a taste for psalmody that has long been forgotten in our world. I imagined him quite well, a kid with dark curls, at the center of a circle of children as dark and curled as he was, conscientiously repeating after his masters, again and again, with no vocal inflection but with all his fervor, passages taken from ancient religious texts. In this way he had been able to lodge at the heart of his book everything needed to evoke a complaint, a moan, a somewhat uncouth appeal intended to bespeak danger, suffering. In short, a cry.

And that was it. Nothing else emerged from the page; it did not respond to my blandishments. My soliloquy remained a dead letter. The essence of the message was no easier to grasp in the phonic elements of the text than in the graphic signs . . .

I came to wonder whether I hadn't been too timid, whether I shouldn't test hypotheses more audacious and imaginative than those I'd thus far thought up, which were, ultimately, rather ordinary.

Maybe I shouldn't confine myself to the voice alone? When one transmits a message, the voice is only one element among many others; the rest of the body is heavily involved in the act of communication. Why should syllables be forever doomed to be the slaves of the gullet? I felt a new task had been assigned me: to play my body as if it were a musical instrument, to try to perform a kind of graft that would allow me to interpret this page not with my voice alone, but with my whole person. It some-times happens that language, exhausted, calls upon another mode of expression to transmit what it itself can no longer say. Unfortunately, I had no idea how to proceed: should I mime the text, dance it, sing it?

And, as a matter of fact, I discovered that with its odd punc-tuation and short paragraphs, the text assumed, irrefutably, the appearance of musical score. The word *resolution*, over which I had too quickly skimmed the preceding day – wasn't it, with its four notes (D, C, A, C), like a discreet oboe harmony that was to set me on the right path? Perhaps I had to pursue this trail, which was certainly worth some attention, all the way to the end.

Thanks to Sophie, who had forced me to fill in some of the gaps in my education (which had been considerably less ne-glected in the domain of the arts than in that of science), I knew various musical settings, and first of all a central scene in *A Masked Ball* (in Karajan's version – the only one that did not offend the ears of my imperious teacher), where it is the music alone that simultaneously magnifies the text and reveals its true meaning. But how was I to find the music that was hidden be-hind the words, that revealed how the words should be used?

Maybe here things were the way they were in another opera from which Sophie had once sung me an all-too-brief extract, in which, with a rare and marvelous economy, the same docile arrangement of syllables constituted both the score and the li-bretto . . . Perhaps here too, certain syllables had to be read as if they were notes? Perhaps the message had been inscribed in the form of a melody?

Reconstituting all that seemed to me a promising enterprise, and one that was worth trying out right away.

Very quickly, I succeeded in jotting down in my notebook a

large number of A's, accompanied by some E's and F's, very few C's or D's, and even fewer G's. But how could I get a message, no matter how condensed, out of that? I tried again and again, to no avail – it was beyond me. There was probably something I hadn't fully mastered, or had badly assimilated, in the method I was using. Weary, I let the idea go. Not without a sigh of regret.

More stubborn than I was, the text clung to its indecipherable clarity.

Should I stop there, and admit that I'd covered all the terrain that separates the voice from writing and come up with nothing? That was impossible, of course.

But had I in fact done what I should have?

Once again, doubt and concern began to grip me: what error, what oversight had I been guilty of that led me to such a pitiful result?

Maybe it was simply that my voice was not suitable for the purpose? Too high or too low? Or was it a banal question of enunciation, of accent, or God knows what? I had had to endure, in elementary school, many more or less well-intentioned remarks about the alleged peculiarities of my pronunciation: one teacher found my *o*'s too open, and another found my *e*'s too short and too closed. I'd never paid any attention to these comments. Wrongly, no doubt. Wasn't this the moment to recall them and try to acknowledge my mistakes? But how?

The best thing was probably to have someone else read this page, to try it with a gullet very different from mine. It would hardly be surprising, after all, if an alien, expert mouth were able to bring out of the text truths that an excessively anxious reader is incapable of perceiving. Therefore I had immediately to find someone who would lend me his voice, as other people, in other places, had sometimes lent me their pens. And then that would also give me an opportunity to get out of this tête-à-tête that was only increasing my gloom. On someone else's face, I could follow the sequence of feelings (surprise, anger, incredulity, concern) that would not fail to appear there, and compare in this regard my own face with his.

Naturally, I was thinking first of all of Sophie. Yes, together the game would be more fun to play, and we would not be so overmatched. We could compare ideas, hatch new ones, move much faster in testing our hypotheses. And the text would finally surrender and allow itself to be read.

But I couldn't make up my mind to do it. I'm not sure why, but the more I struggled with my page, the more I felt the imperious need not to involve Sophie in any way in this venture. I was afraid of what her reaction might be, undeniably. It was far from sure that she would find this text as important as I did, or that she would see in it something mysterious and suitable for metaphysical meditation. To tell the truth, I was almost certain that the contrary would be true. I had only to recall a few brief, recent scenes that had set us violently in opposition to each other: every time, she had taken pleasure in sweeping away with a single word, as if they were negligible details, everything on which I had tried, for years, to base my thought. But things might turn out even worse, if, as I feared when I looked at this text, she entered the fray without immediately winning a victory. For in moments of disappointment or anger, she was capable of falling into glum, murky silences that were impossible to penetrate and which I had no wish to encounter.

It would be better for sure to call on one of my neighbors: the one upstairs, for instance, whose married life I was getting to know quite well (rather better than I wanted to), and whose nervous, staccato footsteps I sometimes heard just before dawn. Unfortunately, at this time my relations with the neighbors were not of a kind that authorized such little exchanges of favors; they still mistrusted me a bit, and I felt as if I were on probation. Sophie had even told me, without being willing to tell me where she'd gotten this information, that I had no sooner moved into my apartment than I had won the reputation of being a 'neurasthenic' . . .

As for bringing in a stranger, an actor, for instance, who might be able to concentrate all his talent on this single page, that was out of the question. I couldn't see myself telling this whole story, right from its incredible beginning, to someone of whose discretion I could not be sure.

This consideration sufficed to reveal to me the absurdity of my last hypothesis. It is clear that people don't transmit a secret through the mediation of a third person who might be tempted to divulge it, or worse yet, keep it for himself. Moreover, was it possible seriously to imagine being told a secret otherwise than in the solitude of a tête-à-tête?

It was clear that I had been mistaken all along the way, that this long detour through language, the voice, the body, and the rest had only further blurred the path and ultimately forced me into pointless wanderings. The supposed importance of giving voice to the dumb text, perversely suggested in the book's first word, was only another mirage!

Do I now dare to admit it? Frankly, I wasn't really upset that the key to my enigma didn't lie in that area. If, as I had every reason to suppose, the message I was looking for was spiritual in nature, it was very unlikely that the author would have chosen, in order to transmit it, the spoken word, which is connected with the relatively crude sense of hearing, rather than writing, which is inseparable from the most noble of the senses, sight.

Moreover, while I was declaiming the text, watching the deformations of my mouth and my face (they were so grotesque that they sometimes made me feel like angrily throwing my shoe at the mirror), I had not been able to keep from thinking that the transition from the hieratic rigor of writing to the hazards of the spoken word, whatever attraction it might otherwise have for me, clearly had something regressive about it.

7

So I had to get moving again. Moving forward, of course. The question was how, and where to go. I had just been through my text, from front to back, several times, and in every direction, without succeeding in grasping it.

Then I had a new idea, which was, actually, quite simple.

To move forward, to finally make the barriers yield, I clearly had to move backwards, once again, all the way to the beginning. To go back to the primordial element, the words. But since words, like air or water, present a certain resistance to anyone trying to pass through them, I must not hesitate, in order to break this resistance, to break the words themselves. No longer try to seduce them or attract their condescending sympathy by my repeated, clumsy errors. On the contrary, I had to scrutinize them to the point of destroying them. Strike them, if necessary. With great pickaxe blows. In order to make the seams of gold appear. And if that was not enough, then still more refined modes of torture (to which I would be forced, despite my reluctance, to resort) would end up making them confess their secret truths.

Therefore I went back to the words on this page, taking them one by one.

First, as if they were the pearls of a necklace that one rolls gently between one's fingers, I examined them. Then I started dividing them into syllables. In the hope that from these resonant debris, if I could grip them tightly enough, would ultimately emerge illuminating glosses.

I was convinced that my quest would become more serious, because this time it was going to take its models right from mythology: like Isis gathering up the scattered fragments of her brother-husband, I too would reassemble, syllable by syllable, the elements of a dissimulated corpus.

In doing so, I also remembered certain procedures cherished by the poets of ancient India and Rome. They sought to reproduce, to suggest, tirelessly, the sonorities of a single name: that of the divinity or hero whom they wished to honor. It even happened sometimes that the word that was the subject, the key, of a whole text did not appear overtly even once. Could that be the case here?

But all my efforts yielded only very unstable results that immediately evanesced, without having illuminated me at all.

Then I resolved to attack the syllables themselves. And I did so at first with a kind of cold fury. As if there had suddenly awakened in me, arising from some very distant place, a desire to destroy, a spirit of revolt against the violence of rules and their arbitrariness. Each syllable was thus promptly denuded, reduced to the simple letters that composed it. I spelled these letters one by one, erased them, brought them back again, constantly watching for the moment when I could move from the simple typographic sign to the message. Other people, who had not hesitated to adorn their slender songs with anagrams, had succeeded in reading an allegory of the Idea in Maurice Scève's *Délie*, and in transforming 'Florence Nightingale' into 'flit on, cheering angel.'

It was a bottomless vortex. But at times it offered glimpses of a splendid horizon. Thanks to the feeling of omnipotence it evoked in me, I was able to see language with new eyes. Words, syllables, and letters were finally freed from all the questionable connections they had acquired in their previous lives: liberated from the tangle that usually restrains them, they seemed to have just been born. I was thus sent back to the rudiments, plunged back into the time when I was first discovering, with both astonishment and delight, the order of the letters and their countless combinations. The alphabet itself appeared in its most affable aspect, and no longer attired in its endless frills and flounces.

This time, I was sure that I could reach out and touch, beyond all the figures and ornaments, the unsuspected suppleness of language. An intoxicating feeling, against which Mr. Raymond, my dear old teacher (who, in order to improve his teaching, had spent most of his life ferrying back and forth between the Larousse and the Littré dictionaries), had said to me one day, during one of our private conversations, in that strange African accent that then so strongly impressed me (as sharp and harsh as you could imagine, he reminded me of one of my uncles): 'Beware of those moments when you feel that words are getting away from you, or rather going off the rails . . .'

I already knew, because I had discovered it myself during earlier meditations, that words bear death within them without seeming to do so, that only the void is there in the middle of all these supposed appearances. But now, it was much worse: all I had to do was to examine an utterance, no matter what it was, with a certain degree of attention, in order to perceive within it, stubbornly present, and gnawing on its very heart, negation. In a word, with my eyes constantly peeled, I began to discern exactly what you see when you humbly agree to pursue the expressible all the way to the end.

In doing so, I didn't think I was destroying, but on the contrary, creating. Everything suggested that I was participating in a mystery, the mystery of Nature itself: the decomposition of an object into its elements in order to recompose it in a different form. Thus, for me, words were also involved in the fundamental cycle of death and resurrection.

I was not unhappy with this result.

Alas, as satisfying as it seemed to me (for it allowed me to settle some old scores), it was obviously not the result I was expecting that day.

My perplexity grew.

The more I read, the more (the key to the text remaining beyond my grasp) I got mired down. I had manipulated this page like a lump of clay, I had sliced it up into its tiniest bits. Every path I had taken seemed to be blocked. If there was a message, I now had to admit that it escaped me.

I felt dejection rising up in me, along with its bitter creaking.

To some extent, I was probably to blame for this whole affair: why had I so naïvely yielded to my romantic love of mystery and enigmas? Afflicted with the strange malady that consists in seeing difficulties invisible to ordinary mortals (a form of madness that an indulgent friend once assured me, no doubt with the intention of consoling me, was as rare as it was fruitful), I had plunged headlong into an obstacle that might be merely imaginary.

It was no longer the time to be starting out on another wrong track. It was urgent that I find some way of keeping from getting lost.

I thought of all the people who had had more luck with their readings than I had had, and who had been able to find right away what they were looking for in their books, and even a little bit more. And I couldn't help expressing a few regrets as I reflected on this. Just think how much trouble the guy would have spared me, had he simply had the good grace to commit the careless mistake made by the French consul, a writer in his spare time, who once sent his superiors a coded letter and put the key in the same envelope! Why didn't that letter, rather than one or another of his works decked like flags with gaudy colors (but in my humble opinion far less emblematic), become a model for all those who use a pen?

Alas, my author, although not hemmed in by the obligations of diplomatic correspondence, seemed on the contrary to have taken care to lock everything up tight: no foreword, no preamble, no introduction, no preface. Not a marginal remark or note anywhere. Ah, if only I had in front of me the manuscript of this damned page! Then I would surely have been able to see right through my unknown author: by examining the traces of his hand, by scrutinizing the trajectory he had imposed on each of the characters he had shaped, by analyzing his way of dividing them up and putting them together. No living person is capable of keeping a secret; he betrays himself in countless ways, and without even having to open his lips . . .

But like those ancient monuments whose haughty, massive presence doesn't care a fig about any justification and gives no thought to seeking the approbation or complicity of the speechless passerby, here the text displayed itself naked, in its anonymity.

Should I continue to do battle against my unknown author?

Didn't he resist too obviously the role of a messenger come from a foreign land, a role which, in the expectation of some kind of glad tidings, I had tried to foist on him?

For an instant, I had the impression that I saw him in front of me, just as he was putting the finishing touches on his address. With a satisfied smile, finding in advance a tribute in each of our failures, he imagined us, all of us who were going to read him, as a flock of pigeons wheeling around a weathercock: they turn, they turn, they turn, and then, exhausted, they fall.

I even wondered, now, why I had let myself be led so far. Should I see, in my refusal to open my eyes and see the disappointing reality of this page, an instinctive defense against the shock that greater perceptiveness would have threatened to produce? It wouldn't have been the first time.

These few sentences, to be sure, were not completely devoid of minor attractions. But nothing strong. Nothing that overwhelms or seduces. None of those images with voluptuous or violent consequences, none of those sparks that give you the illusion, even if fugitive, of discovery. And then, neither my life nor my honor, so far as I knew, depended on this text. Only a misplaced desire to play Oedipus had made me take a very mediocre scribbler for a Sphinx.

No, it had become clear that these words didn't mean anything more than they said: all the rest was literature.

8

And so I found myself, apart from certain details (not all of them negligible, however), very close to my starting point. Or more precisely, rather far behind it. Oh, yes! I had set out, a dashing knight sure of a quick victory, in order to save the meaning an evil sorcerer held captive in the toils of his rhetoric, and now it was I who was, at the end of a tortuous treasure hunt, caught. Nabbed, hostage, undone, crushed, trampled underfoot, in a word, vanquished. To get out of this, I couldn't count on any very unlikely outside intervention. An embarrassing turn of events!

If reading – like writing, like speaking – is an act of love, then I had arrived, with this book, at that pale time of the night when lovers, exhausted but not yet satisfied, hesitate to go at it again and dream only of a mouthful of cold water.

My curiosity, which had been so lively a moment earlier, had now dissipated. The words, too long scrutinized, interrogated, importuned, had ended up becoming opaque for me; they had withdrawn, sullenly, into their shells.

I had every reason to leave this miserable page to its fate. I had grappled with it so much, I had chewed on it and ruminated on it so much, that it left me with a strange taste in my mouth, acerbic and full of bitterness, and I didn't know how to get rid of it.

My reading had transformed itself (depending on my contradictory intuitions) into a calculation, prayer, music, rite, sacrifice. More solidly set on its foundations than the walls of Jericho, the page always held its own. Every time I had thought I was about to grasp it, the meaning had evaporated. If it is true that vision is the art of seeing the invisible, well, I have to recognize that I had just provided, in a magisterial manner, the proof of my complete blindness.

Like those peoples who decorate everything at great expense on days of defeat (for otherwise the humiliation would be too much to bear), I sought a final consolation. I found it, not without difficulty: By imagining that I had simply been put under a spell. Yes, something like a curse. The same one that, an Egyptologist friend of mine had once told me without cracking a smile, pursues the excavator who dares to let into the tomb of a pharaoh (normally destined to remain eternally dark) the first ray of light.

There was no longer any point, of course, in calling Flauzac. To tell him what? I didn't give a damn about his book: I was even ready to throw it in the wastebasket, once and for all. And then I didn't want to show my friend how thoroughly I had let myself be had by what could only be, so far as he was concerned, a joke. If I had to talk to someone, it would be Sigmund, or François. Sure, the Allobrogian and the Crow, who, like poor Charles, had escaped the politico-literary phalanstery of our early years in Paris: there were originally seven of us, a group of indefatigable dreamers, who had quickly been joined by a couple of bohemian types who considered themselves, as propriety then required, to be fighting on behalf of the Third World. They would laugh at my book and its fussiness, because (in their case, lucidity was not incompatible with fun) they found everything amusing, which justified the name of *fearless thinkers* that they had once proposed (unsuccessfully) as a name for our group.

Suddenly, a memory from that period in my life came back to me.

It was the time when we were proclaiming that it was from Asia that salvation, or rather Salvation (a belief that didn't last long, or at least hardly any longer than any of the others that had preceded it and that were characterized by equally great discernment . . .) would come. I had undertaken to prepare my spirit for this advent. Through reading, of course, and through an accelerated course of study on Oriental wisdom.

I had then been struck by certain practices of Zen Buddhism. I immediately saw in them a curiously close resemblance to another, less exotic tradition, that of the Greek Cynics: Among other things, there was the rule that the future disciple was to be shaken up, knocked off his pins by sarcasm, insult, and even violence if necessary. It was especially, if I remember correctly, in the school of Rinzaï (whom some people call Lin Tsi), that distinguished itself, in this domain, by its unorthodox methods: the blows delivered by Rinzaï/Lin Tsi's stick were almost as famous as his scornful belches . . .

In this way, the novice was asked questions (koans) that apparently had no answers, at least no logical answers. These utterances in the form of enigmas had greatly pleased me at the time; they made me think of some of the most eloquent of the surrealist butterflies. The first koan, all by itself, required whole days of meditation:

You know the sound of two hands clapping, but what is the sound of one hand clapping?

But there were many, many others:

What makes you answer when you are called?

Or:

What did your face look like before you were born?

The poor disciple labored on these for a long time. His mind trapped in a genuine dead end, his reason disarmed, he ended up entering a state of extreme tension that was supposed to promote illuminations. Thus eventually he became capable of apprehending reality at a single glance, beyond oppositions, beyond contradictions.

And what if my anonymous author was an adept of these shock-technique educational methods? What if he belonged to that fringe of people that know where the straight path is, not the broad, spacious, shady path that is open to anyone who comes along, but the other one, rough, stony (or perhaps sandy), and full of obstacles? A knowledge he would have gained, I thought immediately, from lessons received very far from here.

Thus contrary to what usually happens, it was not my author who had led me off on exotic wanderings; it was I who, starting from my own memories, had to follow the chain all the way back, and reconstitute the expeditions during which the chain had been able to shape itself. But at the point where I currently was, persuaded that I was approaching the end of my trials, this sudden inversion of the roles hardly troubled me at all.

I even took pleasure, now, in imagining my author as a traveler: fascinated since childhood by the numberless promises contained in the word 'departure,' liking to taste again, through the pages of a few great works leafed through tirelessly, the taste of salt and wind, the smell of the tides, of the ships' caulking heated white-hot by the August sun, and all the strong odors of old harbors. Realizing rather late in life his old dream, but now wanting to measure himself against the universe in the hope of becoming one with it, he would one day have embarked, alone, on one of those steamers that, after weeks of sailing, unloads in distant ports loads of voyagers dressed in white.

Foregoing visits to mausoleums zigzagged with cracks, he would have walked about aimlessly. In Benares, he would have arrived by chance, one night when the moon was full, in the Deer Park (without even knowing that that was where the Buddha had given his first sermon) and meditated there all night. In the suburbs of Colombo, he would have contemplated, among the coconut trees, the bungalows and verandahs overflowing with flowers. Then, tired of wandering, one morning he would have decided to stop.

Secretly searching, perhaps, a kind of punishment, but with the certainty that he would emerge from it regenerated, he would have spent long months studying with some venerable master, who would have allowed him, because of his rigor and patience, to approach the Four Noble Truths and the Eightfold Path. On this occasion, he would also have discovered the virtues of the koan. Perhaps he would even have been called upon to meditate on the famous koan of the lances: *Seven times, you have turned your tongue in your mouth before speaking: how many lances do you break when you cry out?*

And it is at the moment of finishing his book – this book in which his wanderings and the stages of his awakening were no doubt to be narrated in detail – that he would have recalled, with a certain remaining affection, the methods of his old master, and had the idea of borrowing them. Then, wanting to select his readers before being read by them, he would have decided to test their strength and determination, as he had himself once been put to the test. The only reader he would approve was one who did not allow himself to be deceived and who knew how to understand more than what was said.

So now everything would start to become clear.

The key to the enigma was not, as I had too long thought, in the form or arrangement of the words, the syllables, or the letters, but elsewhere: in the way one had to look at the page, which appeared before my eyes as it had been transformed by my curiosity.

The alleged initial paradox? An ancient technique of tough

pedagogy, hardly updated, in order to create, perhaps, a kind of halo of surprise, a vague replica of the *distantiation* long cherished by our elders.

The door slammed in the visitor's face? A rather odd way of striking, as in the theater, the three blows that announce that the play is about to begin. Or better yet, a rite of welcome, a sign of complicity: a pledge, for anyone who showed himself worthy of it, of the friendship that would soon be established, and that might continue, growing stronger from page to page. Behind the rigid gestures of rejection, a discreetly outlined invitation had to be discerned.

One thing then became obvious: the only pertinent response to the initial injunction was to pay no attention to it and to pursue without hesitation the reading that it seemed to prohibit. I had been right, in short, to read this page as a provocation. But it was a provocation to move forward.

I was more than a little proud of having gotten so far. It was fortunate, too, that the solution was this one: so much simpler than any of the others I'd conceived. Like Ulysses facing the Sirens, but without needing to stop my ears, I was now in a position to meet my examiner's questions with the serene irony of the person who knows what's up.

This was certainly not the first time, in the history of human relations, that signs had to be completely inverted in order to find the meaning of a message. Professional diplomats know something about that!

But this solution was probably too simple to occur to me immediately. It required a long and laborious conquest. That's how it is. Some people can find the path right away and never get lost in all the detours and bifurcations. But I, of course, took the longest path first, as if I feared nothing so much as arriving too quickly at the destination (is that because I suspect that no one is waiting for me there?). As pointless as it may seem, my herme-neutic tenacity had for me the bitter taste of victory.

And then (why not openly admit it from now on?) I was curious to find out what was going to come after the remarks that had so long stopped me in my tracks. This page that I had up to this point obstinately refused to turn over, for it seemed to me blocked like a door on rusty hinges, onto what would it open?

I was convinced that a single glance would suffice, a simple quick look that would put me on the path to a genuine revela-tion.

Perhaps I was going to comprehend abruptly that I already had my educator, my liberator, the author whose work, like a luminous point in the middle of an immense, obscure mass, was going to show me the way from this point on. Perhaps this was finally the book that I had so long dreamed of encountering, the unique book, unknown to booksellers, not listed in any cata-log, of which even the most knowledgeable librarians had never heard, and which was going to speak to me alone.

Like the neophyte on the threshold of the sacred grotto, I could not suppress a shiver of fear. For I knew, from many ac-counts, the delights as well as the dangers connected with this kind of encounter. I even recalled the story (a true one, I've been told) of the bookstore employee who one day found in his shop, high on a top shelf, among old German books forgotten there for ages, a volume of Jean-Paul (an author he had never read, but whose excessively short name intrigued him, and on whom he had taken, a priori, a sort of crush): he began to translate it, and the result at which he arrived seemed to him so fascinating that he immediately decided to devote the rest of his life to exploring other German Romantic writers, on whom he became the best-known specialist.

I took the time to savor this moment of hope. To the point of forgetting (but of course I was not, at the time, aware of the importance of this unfortunate oblivion) another of my old family precepts (somewhat less solemnly transmitted than the earlier ones, but just as weighty), the one that enjoined me always to retain, even in the midst of the greatest happiness, a place for sadness.

THIRD MOVEMENT

If your mind wants to conceal
The finest things you think,
Tell me, who can stop you
From remaining silent?
    – Maynard

The best way
to be understood is to let
everything be divined.
    – Reverdy

9

Pardon me. I am going to have to ask you a question that is less indiscreet (how can I tell you this without jolting you?) than incongruous. Yes, that's what you'll think it is: incongruous. But in my view, it is indispensable. So here it is: ARE YOU SURE THIS IS THE BOOK YOU WANTED TO READ?

Make sure, please, that there is no confusion on your part. For you may not know this, but there is nothing less rare than this kind of error. So many books are published, and they resemble each other so much, that it's all too easy, if you're not on your guard, to mistake one author for another. A simple letter added, moved, omitted, here and there, is sometimes enough. Be sure that you are not doing that very thing, at this very moment. You have, you know, plenty of time.

What, you find this new injunction surprising?

It even wounds you a little?

You're not the kind of person, you say, who embarks upon a reading capriciously, and still less on the basis of a vague homonymy. You've considered for a long time before choosing this work, before arriving at this page.

Well done! Since that's the case, you can ignore these words and move on.

But you – yes, you, who have just taken a worried look at the dust jacket to check the book's content, and discovered, not without concern, that it is not (contrary to what you took to be well-established custom) entirely in agreement with what you expected, you, who are having doubts, even if they are fleeting, right now – don't wait any longer to get rid of this book.

It's not good that you read it.
So dump it. Or better yet, throw it as far away as you can.
It may, however, already be too late.

Hardly had I finished examining the peculiarities of the dust jacket (which had allowed me to discover, instead of the usual information, a poor-quality vignette reproducing, in black and white, a picture I could not immediately identify with precision, but which I thought I could attribute to a Flemish painter: Hobbema, Bouts, or rather, some needy epigone who succeeded in making a name for himself by shamelessly imitating both of them), before I was stricken with a sort of nausea.

With great difficulty, I managed to suppress it.

After having been banged around so much, so shaken, I had dreamed of a warm welcome. I would have liked to experience at least once the joy of the shipwrecked man who, thrown up naked and exhausted, after drifting for a long time at sea, on an unknown shore, suddenly sees his salvation in the eyes of a princess with smooth, white arms, whom a compassionate divinity has sent to meet him! Then I would have thought my obstinacy suitably rewarded.

But here again, nothing happened as it did in the stories that had occupied my childhood. Instead of the shock, the spark, the sign, (whatever form it might take) that I was hoping for, this was the kind of wretched sop I was thrown: another layer of bark when I was expecting the sapwood, another layer of skin when I thought I was touching the heart!

This page, which I had so hesitated to turn, this page where I had still been hoping, just a moment earlier, to discover torrents of milk and rivers of honey, this page whose content, had it been what I wanted, could have (I was ready for this) changed the course of my life, explained nothing, yielded nothing, opened onto nothing: it offered me, instead of a revelation, another warning.

Exactly as if my author, satisfied (and this is, to tell the truth, an old habit among literary men, which they are not about to give up) with the idea he'd thought up for this opening page, had immediately felt an urgent need to do an encore. With a difference, however, that I could not fail to notice. Neither the language nor the tone, as is probably fitting when one has passed onto the other side, were the same: the earlier curt arrogance had suddenly given way, at least in appearance, to a kind of humility.

To be sure, this way of proceeding was not, in itself, always blameworthy. I also sometimes took a form of pleasure, and even a sort of delight, in the recurrence, the repetition, the insistent return, at short intervals, of the same words, the same sentences, the same page, if need be. But this still had to be justified in some way within the general design. Was that the case here? I was not at all convinced that it was.

Nevertheless, I tried to take my author seriously, to understand what he was doing. What led him to make himself so jealously the jailer of his own writings? Why did he redouble his precautions in this way, surrounding what ought to be the heart of his book, as ancient strategists surrounded their fortresses, with a second line of defense? What was the object of all this protection? His book? His (hypothetical) reader? Or simply himself? And what was he protecting it from, after all?

If I set aside the notion that it might be simply a mystification, I had to admit that this repetition could not be gratuitous. It was supposed to say something, something important, to those who had made their way past the first barrier. But what?

Perhaps the author, getting ready to lift the veil covering a mystery that unprepared minds could not witness without risks, simply wanted to keep us from being shocked. He was in a position to know that what he was going to say was not at all comforting. In that case, wouldn't it be perfectly legitimate to take a few precautions? He didn't want just anyone following him into the dark universe he had explored and from which he had brought us some heartbreaking discoveries. Restricting in every way he could the number of those who were to be allowed access to this revelation, making sure at least that they were capable of continuing onward to the rest of his message: after all, there was nothing unacceptable about his stubborn search for 'the happy few.' The accumulated experience of predecessors must have made it clear to him how difficult it is to be a prophet: he probably wouldn't have dared even open his lips had he been able to foresee the thoughtlessness of many of those who were to follow him and take him as their master . . .

However, one thing puzzled me: In justifying himself, why did he allude to the errors resulting from homonymy? I'd never seen that one before. This sudden concern about identity – what sense did that make coming from a writer who had expressly chosen not to reveal his own identity? Was it carelessness? Inconsistency? I was well on my way to a new series of hypotheses.

Maybe he wanted, by means of a provocation almost as paradoxical as the one in his initial address, to pique my curiosity again, to tell me that I shouldn't stop there, to reignite my interest in a page that, as he was well aware, could only have disappointed me: thus he was encouraging me not to stand staring on the shore, but to move beyond the apparent contradiction, to pursue the voyage of exploration upon which I had already embarked.

But maybe instead he wanted to make me understand that the anonymity was merely fictitious. When writing books was not yet a widely admired activity (something we find hard to imagine today), many authors resorted, in order to conceal their names, to a variety of artifices, but these were never very difficult to see through. Perhaps he too, far from really intending to remain anonymous, was counting on people guessing who he was. He probably had done everything he could so that people would do just that. Parts of his name, dissolved like a handful of salt in a pond, were surely present somewhere in his text. A reader who knew this, if he were able to detect a few of the tricks (among the most elementary of all those included in the art of playing with words), should be able to find it.

I even wondered whether, behind all his little schemes, his feigned precautions, there was not also a certain amount of bitterness. In reality, my scribbler was furious at the idea that I didn't understand his hints. It was simply because I didn't know him, because I was unfamiliar with his habits. What he would have liked, no doubt, was that I should approach him only after I had been duly humbled and prepared to kneel before him. A persistent rumor was supposed to have told me the name, which had become a password, of this great, underestimated man who, at his little farm on the banks of the Ardèche, cultivated his anonymity with as much love as he cultivated his begonias. One evening, after dinner, a dear friend would have gravely confided to me his opinion of this rare book, of which he would finally have succeeded in acquiring, after months of fruitless searching, a single copy. Thus I would have discovered that this was a secret, powerful book, the object of a regular cult on the part of a small group of fervent devotees: they reread it, meditated on it, and drew their sustenance from it. Intrigued and already seduced, and above all eager to participate, I would have engaged willingly, and even with a certain enthusiasm, in all the rituals that would make it possible for me to enter the brotherhood. In that event, my enthronement would not have happened secretly, nor, as was in fact the case, as a result of a simple accident . . .

On the other hand, I said to myself, if you're so interested in avoiding any risk of being misunderstood, isn't the best way to do that just to keep quiet?

But there you had it – he wasn't keeping quiet. Or rather, he hadn't kept quiet.

Since I had imagined he had some familiarity with Zen, I was astonished that he had not been inspired, as so many others have been, by Liang Kai's painting in which one sees a patriarch laughing bitterly as he tears up a manuscript and throws the pieces to the wind. My author had probably not gone far enough in the process of initiation: he had not been able to master the form of communication favored by the Buddha: silent communication.

So he had resigned himself to this simulacrum.

As if something he could not resist (and which I had often noticed in literary men of a quite different stamp) urged him simultaneously to speak out and to dissimulate, to provoke and to disappoint.

Mentally, I attempted to reconstitute his dilemma (it wasn't hard: all I had to do was put myself in his place). He had to satisfy two incompatible desires. To write: in order to avoid seeing his life bend and then stagger under the weight of the words that had piled up inside and threatened to undermine it; and also in order to break, at least partially, the isolation to which keeping silent had led him. But at the same time, there was a remaining, obsolete fear: he had to conceal, veil his writing, in order to evade the dangers it might bear within it. The need to produce a work thus collided with the impossibility of giving this work a satisfactory content.

I had already encountered authors (what point would there be in naming them?) who, convinced that literature was only an art of variation, managed, over the years, to cobble together something resembling an oeuvre by constantly rewriting the same book. I was afraid that this time I had come across a rarer, and still stranger, specimen: an author who accepted the fact that his book was reducible to a single page, ever begun, never finished!

The absurdity of all this soon cooled my anger. Soon, all that remained was a great, irrepressible desire to laugh. For what had begun with prohibition and threats, looking like a tragedy, was becoming, following a clearly marked path (that had long since been blazed and marked), a farce. Obviously, my first impulse had been the right one, and I should have stuck to it. This whole business had smelled, right from the start, like a mystification: this character didn't have even the shadow of a secret, and his problem was not so much his relationship with me as his relationship with himself.

I was ready to recognize that my expectations had been excessive and my hopes ludicrously inflated. This is, in fact, an old habit of mine, and one in which I still indulge. For a long time, my life consisted of these unreasonable hopes, these necessarily (and nastily) disappointed expectations. I constantly had to throw myself into exploring some new domain, and every time it was a genuine expedition from which I brought back at most a bit of nostalgia. Why did I let this unknown person harass me, push me to the end of my rope? I ought to know, after all, that the thing (how else to call it?) I am looking for is neither in the books I've read nor in the ones I plan to read. It could only be in books that I can't even conceive and that I will probably never, no matter how hard I try, come across.

In one of the circles of Dante's *Inferno*, there is a particularly badly treated category of sinners: the people to whom divine benevolence had graciously given everything they needed to be happy, and who, instead of using these gifts to enjoy as much happiness as they could, spent their lives torturing themselves.

Was I still capable of turning the page, moving on? This no longer had even the savor of a forbidden fruit. The scales had fallen from my eyes, and I couldn't help seeing something morbid in the artificially maintained suspense.

I was on only the second page, and already I was beginning to feel, within myself, a painful sensation of emptiness. Probably analogous to that which so many other people, it is said, discover only once they've arrived at the end of a book: when the author, who at the outset had gotten his claws into the belly of the reader (who, paralyzed by surprise, had let him do it) has finished sucking out of it, in little gulps, whatever juice it is that he needs to pursue his enterprise.

In the drowsiness that now overcame me, I was thinking again about Poe, about that strange story in which we see an artist who paints a portrait of his very young wife; the picture is so lifelike and resembles her so closely that when he has completed it, his wife is dead: the portrait drew its life from that of its model.

it is must this be emphasized again for those very few in number at least I hope who may actually have failed to notice or who on the contrary despite my repeated warnings pretend to be unaware of it it is of course at this precise moment that your adventure will have begun and don't try to tell me that you won't succeed I assure you that you are surprised by this everything will be done without violence of any kind and with your full assent someone whose ultimate intentions you may not know for he will not have had the time to unveil them to you in their entirety will have taken up residence here and in your life and simultaneously in a movement whose perfect reversibility you have never had a chance to gauge with such precision you will have penetrated into his so long as you are able to keep your eyes fixed on him as you are doing at this very moment he will display for you tirelessly his store of signs and yet what are you in relation to him and he in relation to you you cannot describe for someone else your respective positions would you say that you are face to face in the classical position of wrestlers who size each other up for a long time before beginning to fight and who fully intend to convey by this silent message that they will go all out wouldn't you rather be like runners side by side on the starting line, or traveling companions ready to confront together what promises to be a difficult crossing it is not yet time for you to make a decision on this point you will decide later on when you have succeeded in getting a better look at the face of the one who has come to meet you and who for the moment is as you see him only a sketchy silhouette which you are also for him this game could go on a long time if one of you doesn't reveal himself tradition prescribes that it is he who surrenders first and that is

precisely what before your still incredulous eyes for your distrust
persists and even grows with every line he has just done

It was easy for me to stop reading there. And not only because of a new wave of poorly controlled anger.

After this block of text in which all punctuation had been omitted, I once again ran into a big blank space on the page. I took advantage of it. I needed to recover from the effort I had just made to find my bearings in this verbal magma, which was probably intended to be as thick as a dark forest.

So the author had found a new way to intimidate me. A way to discourage me, and at the same time increase my anger. A way more insidious than the earlier ones: this time, by playing on legibility, by intentionally clouding the presentation of his message! Thus, after being arrogant and humble, here he was choosing (the third line of defense – but there was no guarantee that it would be the last – in an apparatus elaborated with greater care than I had at first thought) to be obscure.

Perhaps I should have taken advantage of this opportunity to slip away discreetly. Wasn't it high time to get out of this mess and put an end to the story of this wretched encounter?

But I continued to be very wary of my fits of anger. It is true that I had some major literary blunders on my record. Episodes that did me no honor. More than once in my youth, and even in more recent times, I had been capricious enough to reject with irritation, calling them *crazy*, *absurd*, or *unintelligible*, texts I later discovered were regarded by a narrow fringe of readers as fundamental models.

To cite only one example, I have still not been able to forget (and probably won't for a long time yet, since despite my efforts, the echo still makes itself heard occasionally, as I had just seen) how surprised I had initially been, and then offended, shocked, outraged, the first time (urged on by a teacher who wanted to complete my education and who was probably also interested in testing my reactions, but who had, in this case – as teachers, whose good intentions sometimes obscure their judgment, tend to do – overestimated my meager adolescent abilities) I read the strange memoir of a voyage, full of hallucinating visions, of a vessel with neither helmsman nor helm along some river or other in America, or the series of adventures, genuinely vertiginous, of a Satanic hero completely absorbed, in a mood of macabre elation, with his apocalyptic battle against God, or, what seemed to me at the time to be worse than all the rest, ill-prepared for it as I was by a couple of years of reading very classical works (among which the 'condemned poems' in Baudelaire's *Les Fleurs du mal* and the delightfully erudite impudence of the deliquescent des Esseintes were the most advanced) for such disconcerting encounters, the inextricable skein of words and sentences feverishly piled up over hundreds and hundreds of pages with very little punctuation or paragraphs by a mysterious writer who had at first appeared (no matter what he might say) less interested in literature than in the lamentable frivolities of high society, and who nevertheless, having dipped in his herbal tea, one day, a small round cake (whose taste and name were still unknown to me, for it was certainly not the kind of pastry my mother used to give me), ended up becoming the writer that all through his narrative he had feared he would never be. Only modesty and the fear of ridicule prevent me from giving further examples, but believe me, my record in this area was a long one and contained quite a few embarrassing gaffes.

That is why I was determined to show the greatest vigilance, to offer an opinion only after mature reflection, and not without a certain caution: in the wake of Flaubert, I had learned (and I repeated this assertion to myself as if it were an incontestable historical truth) that the accusation of illegibility was invented by lazy or timorous critics incapable of making the effort that reading sometimes requires.

And then, so much perseverance on the author's part had succeeded in shaking my confidence. This tenacity in being evasive – what good did he think that was going to do? Was it supposed to spur on my curiosity? Was it a way of preparing the entrance of the true heroes who would soon appear on the stage? I suspected that something major was at stake in these maneuvers, these dodges. At least, they were a sign that there was a difficult admission to make.

An admission that I thought I could reconstitute by using my imagination, as I had earlier reconstituted (with an ease that I have long since lost) the sequence of reasons that had led some of my friends to lie to me on one occasion or another.

Why not imagine, for instance, that my anonymous author from Aubenas had also dreamed (as everyone does these days) of literary glory? He would have regarded with dismayed surprise (analogous to the surprise shown by many venerable mothers when, virtuously waiting to be served at *their* butcher's, they see breaking in ahead of them a young stranger with a low neckline, loftily ignoring the line and its resigned crowding) the ovations received, in the Parisian world of letters, by certain histrionic writers (at least that is the way he, deep in the provinces, had cataloged them, no matter what their merits might be otherwise) whose provocations and eccentricities were feted as so many strokes of genius. Then he who, soaring high above mere fashions, had remained faithful to the flawless classicism of a transparent writing, would have sought to demonstrate his ability to undermine the rules, to mime great violations of them. But he would not have been able to go very far along the path of what could have been a radical aesthetic quest. Perhaps because literary fashions took a long time to reach Aubenas . . .

The innocent man therefore did not know that in this area, where people specialize in torturing the language, in humiliating the word, in destroying the most elementary conventions (the conventions that had for centuries been regarded as sacred by most nations and had amply proved their ability to persist), the passion for outdoing (as if this very persistence served only to exasperate some people's aggressiveness) held sway, and that, even (and perhaps especially) among the most austere publishers, not a single page worthy of the name of *writing* (this word then being equivalent to absolution of every sin), was ever printed, in some years, that did not bear the mark of the invasion of long sequences composed in unknown languages or alphabets, that were not bristling with Chinese characters, Latin, Greek, or Hebrew maxims (sometimes shamefully disfigured, and usually misunderstood), or that carrying along, like a lava flow, clumps of twisted, scorched, and more-than-half melted words, failed to help accentuate the crushing defeat of codes, or to further the typographic chaos of which it was, for the most part, constituted.

In this author, there was nothing of the kind. He had wanted to be subversive, to be sure. By prowling about the edges of the illegible, he had sought to shake up some of my foundations; perhaps he had even hoped, by so doing, to provide me with some rare delight. But he'd stopped short of his goal, not being willing to go all the way to the extreme point of provocation, where the very possibility of meaning fades away and then disappears. He had not dared to inflict on me that brusque and crabby face that even the greatest writers dare to show only at the end of their careers.

Thus, once the initial moment of surprise had passed, I saw displayed on this page (where no thought had been given to playing on the difference between letters, the arrangement of

119

spaces, or the distance between the lines), neither a cascade of portmanteau words, nor neologisms invented for the occasion, nor a deluge of onomatopoeias, nor a tide of monstrous words composed of fifty or a hundred letters.

It was clear, then, that in his view the word and writing had preserved most of their ancient prestige. Convinced that the appearance of a text, its visual aspect, determines its meaning, he had carefully prepared the page's presentation. And because he desired that the course of his discourse not be held up, that it be perceived as a continuous flow, he had simply suppressed periods and commas.

I was about to praise him for this restraint (probably involuntary, for I strongly suspected that it testified, not to his wisdom, but rather to his pusillanimity) when I recalled the title page: there, the boundaries had been openly transgressed. At least that is what I'd thought I'd perceived when I first looked at the book. But since the preceding day I had so often been forced to admit my mistakes and change my way of seeing things that I obviously couldn't stick to this initial impression.

It was time, it seemed to me, to get clear about this. All the more since I also felt, after this incessant slide into uncertainty, the need for an anchorage: something that would finally be solid, to which I could cling. I wanted to know – and this appeared to me a minimal demand – the title of this book. If only to be able, should it prove necessary, to designate it correctly. It seemed absurd to have spent so much time on a volume that I still found doubly mysterious.

Therefore I once again examined the design that spread over the page that was normally reserved for the title.

At first, I thought it was a kind of illumination, like the ones that, on the most precious manuscripts, immediately reveal the content of the passage one is about to read: in the margin, along the top, in a cartouche, in a frontispiece, sometimes simply inserted into the curlicues and flourishes of the initial, or even nestled in the empty spaces that have been carefully provided in the middle of the page, a scene is there, with its picturesque decor and its easily recognizable figures, meticulously composed in order to represent a famous event, a celebrated episode from history or legend. Pinned up among many others over my desk (I had spread around me, at eye level, many images of diverse provenance), were three postcards reproducing such scenes: In one, before his astonished subjects, Nebuchadnezzar is preparing to deliver the children from the fiery furnace; in another, Ghengis Khan, wearing a Bukhara turban, is addressing a large group of believers. On the last, my favorite (because Sophie had sent it to me from Brussels during a brief visit to the Royal Library there), three ladies in their finest clothes surround the dying Philip the Good, while a fourth reads to him.

But that was not the case here: no scene, no figure, no matter what tradition it might belong to, was discernible on this title page.

Was it a purely abstract composition, then, like the interlacing, branching designs that have become the almost inevitable ornament of editions of works from the Orient? Not that, either. What I saw did have to do with typography, but with a strange typography, which was in any case unknown to me.

The title was composed of a series of convoluted capital letters, whose painstaking design seemed intended to resemble, with a touching awkwardness, the appearance of either hieroglyphs (however, I doubt that any of them had ever figured in a cartouche) or Chinese ideograms (but it was clear that these had never adorned any stela).

In fact, the whole thing recalled rather the drawings in children's magazines in which a single figure represents, depending on the angle from which it is viewed, either, in three-quarter profile, the smiling features of a young woman with long, rippling hair, or, in close-up, those of a hideous old woman who looks like a witch and is gap-toothed and cackling to boot. I remember how this image fascinated me. It also worried me, as if it involved me personally. I couldn't understand by what magical operation the ear or the cheek of one of these figures suddenly became the eye or the nose of the other. I hated the witch, of course, and wouldn't have wanted to remain alone with *her* for anything; however, as soon as I rediscovered, by blinking my eyes and turning the drawing every which way, the young woman's lovely, sincere smile, I felt the need to see if the other one was still there. I spent a long time going back and forth between the two silhouettes in this way, constantly fearing, at the very moment when I glimpsed one of them, that I would no longer be able to find the other.

But here, I had followed, one after the other, each of the paths the swarm of letters suggested to me, without arriving at any satisfactory result.

Finally, I realized that I would not be able to manage this by myself. In dealing with a somewhat perverse expert like my author, you had to bring in other experts who were capable of breaking the spell. Among my friends, there were two whom I knew to be better prepared for this sort of task than I was. I ended up deciding to ask their help, but I was resolved, of course, not to tell them anything about what I'd just been through with this book.

I hadn't seen either of them for a long time (I'd been surprised, moreover, by their absence, over a period of several years, from our ritual get-togethers, but our friendship was so old, and so strong, that it survived these eclipses undamaged. François (whom everyone called the Crow, a nickname whose origin we did not know) and old Sigmund (who liked to be called the *Allobrogian* and claimed to be from Vienne) were well-suited to each other: they were both crazy about enigmas, riddles, word puzzles, and conundrums of all kinds. The Crow, whose work in an insurance office in the rue de Prague left him some spare time, liked nothing better than to perfect new brain twisters, which he took pleasure in making as complicated as he could. His inventions could be found quite regularly in certain large-circulation weeklies, which offered them to their readers as beach amusements for the month of August. Once, he had even written for a whole year a regular puzzle column in one of the morning daily papers, called 'The Crow's Cache.' But the best of his discoveries he refused to publish, reserving them for the shrewdness, and the delight, of his closest friends.

The Allobrogian was one of these. Very early on, he had specialized, to the detriment of the medical studies he was never able to complete, in the resolution of this kind of problem. This had given him a mental flexibility and agility he could use in any other domain. One day when he was sitting in a bar, he had begun, as a joke, to explain the other patrons' dreams to them. Word got around. He did it again. People who wanted their dreams interpreted flocked to him. He began to get into it. From that time on, nothing escaped his frenetic passion for interpretation.

I felt the need to put things in order before my friends arrived. My desk was still covered with sheets of paper I'd scribbled on the preceding day while I was searching for my evanescent message. I didn't want them to see those! So I hurriedly picked them up. Then I took them into the bathroom, piled them up in the sink, and, with a pleasure that I made no attempt to hide from myself, I put a match to them. But the smell of burned paper quickly became unbearable, and I had to leave the room before everything was consumed.

The only thing left for me to do was wait.

If only I could have reached Sophie! This would have been the ideal moment to talk with her . . . But where was she? I had to be satisfied with cursing internally, once again, the cruel absurdity of the constraints she had imposed on my love.

Now too tense to be able to undertake the slightest new activity, I ended up resigning myself to going back to my book, which I turned over and over in my hands, mechanically.

This time, it seemed to me very dull.

The binding, which I had not yet had an opportunity to examine, was without originality and even lacked any characteristic that might make it possible to identify it, to assign it a date, a provenance. The page design had obviously been neglected, as if those responsible for it, hurried at the last minute by another sort of urgency, had not thought it possible to put more care into its composition, or even to change a very ill-proportioned justification. As for the typography . . . without being exactly ugly, it seemed not to have been given any more attention than the rest, except perhaps in order to accentuate its oddness. What was the meaning of this choice of squashed letters, exhibiting a defective typeface? I was willing to bet that neither my author nor his publisher had ever heard of Garamond, Baskerville, or Bodoni.

So I thought (maliciously, I confess, but after all, you can't always be brimming over with benevolence) that my oh-so-wary author had missed at least one chance to back his bet, and in such an elegant way.

He claimed he didn't want people to read him? Nothing easier to achieve: had he been less timorous, or better informed about the true ways of bibliophiles, he would have thrown himself into the very expensive project of producing one of those books that have no need to bristle with defenses in order to avoid being read, or rather, are surrounded by protections of another kind, with another kind of dissuasive efficacity.

He would have produced a book loaded with the most precious ornaments. Unique, or almost unique, in the excellence of its paper (one of those soft, supple Japanese papers, which seem to have retained something of the silk rags used in making them), in the quality of its initials, its running heads, colophons, and engravings, and in the choice of the typefaces and the fonts. He might have used, for instance, those marvelous early Renaissance typefaces that so elegantly imitate handwriting: the idea would have come to him when he discovered, in a catalog, a reproduction of a page from Bonaventure Des Périers' *Récréations*.

Of course, particular care would have been given to the binding. He would have entrusted it to some discreet artist, a distant disciple of the great Marius Michel. This artist, immediately enthusiastic about the project, would have chosen the materials, comparing the merits of parchment, basan, vellum, and large-grained Cape morocco, and considered the possible techniques: fillets on the spines, gilding, incrustations, reliefs? Thus he would not have failed to imagine the binding that would best suit the book's content, expressing its soul and respecting its rhythm and its tone.

Such an object, once completed, would have been far too beautiful to be devoted to the elementary and somewhat obscene form of mastication which for some people constitutes the act of reading. On the contrary. Protected from any risk of encountering the kind of ill-mannered gluttons that readers, quite innocently, all too often are, it would have been reserved for the delicate appetite of two or three gourmets, those whose eyes, hungry for beauty and nothing else, are able to derive the most exquisite nourishment from the contemplation of a few beautiful typographical constructions. And, as soon as it had been bound and gilded, discreetly glimmering under its clothing of velvety vellum, more surrounded by respectful consideration than a virgin of yesteryear on her wedding day, it would have immediately found the place that had always been meant for it, clearly the only one worthy of such a perfect work: behind a solid glass pane, sheltered from inappropriate temptations, like a divinity in its temple.

The two friends showed up at my place slightly after the appointed hour; they had had trouble getting into the building and finding my apartment, but this had in no way altered their good humor. Their eyes were sparkling, and the complicity that bound them together showed in their every gesture. They cast a quick glance, which seemed to me quite without amenity, on the collection of old junk that constituted the decor in which I lived. We abridged, as much as possible, the unctuous formalities. Both of them, excited by the idea of a mystery they were fairly confident they could solve, were eager to see the object I had described to them (very summarily, for I lacked the correct words) on the telephone.

So I showed them the book.

They began to pore over the confused mass of ideograms and hieroglyphs and, almost immediately, with a single, identical reaction, and without even having looked at each other, they roared with laughter. A laughter in which irony played a larger part than simple amusement. My uncomfortable air, far from making them stop, only made them laugh the harder.

The Allobrogian was the first to be able to speak. 'Look here,' he cried, 'it's just the word *book*. Sure, there are a few embellishments: a little bazaar Egyptian, accompanied by some cheap Chinese rubbish. And, on top of that, a perfectly commonplace anamorphosis! Amateur work. All you have to do is look at the page from a certain angle . . .'

He had no sooner finished saying this than it jumped out at me. How could I have failed to see it?

Embarrassed, I thanked them. Now I could hardly wait for them to leave, but obviously I couldn't let them see this. I offered tea. They sat down. And, over cups of tea perfumed with bergamot, the conversation dragged on.

As I feared, Flauzac was soon mentioned. Then I discovered that their views regarding our old friend were quite different from mine. Their connections with him had become much looser since the time of *L'Herbe Tendre*, an adventure in which they had both taken part. Sigmund had even been involved in the conception of the project that had caused the enterprise's downfall. It was an episode about which I knew little, for during that period, I was still in Africa, among the blacks, following Monsieur Raymond. He took pleasure in telling me about it in detail, obligingly emphasizing the smallest particularities, which he considered – this was the basis of his whole system of interpretation – the most telling.

It was in January 19——, when the Third International Conference on the Proper Use of Erudition opened in Labouheyre, in the heart of the Landes region, that everything began. The occasion was propitious. The subject chosen by the conference organizers (*Erudition in Fiction: a Blessing and/or an Abuse?*) seemed to have been specially conceived to please our learned friend who, although usually not much inclined to accept this kind of honorific task, had agreed to preside over the opening session and even to deliver (in the presence of the prefect and the rector, who came specifically to hear him) the keynote address.

Flauzac had immediately surprised his audience when, standing on the rostrum, speaking without any notes, in a strong voice that his emotion and the poorly adjusted microphones made unintelligible (completely inaudible, in fact, for the many listeners who had had to jam themselves into the back rows), he declared, by way of introduction, and pronouncing separately, with majestic slowness, each syllable:

My-friends-we-know-from-my-thol-o-gy-that-the-Mu-ses-are-the-sis-ters-and-daugh-ters-of-Mem-o-ry

(a heavy pause, accompanied by a broad smile directed toward the female listeners in the first row, who were perplexed but had already fallen under his spell, for the speaker's lips formed, when pronouncing certain syllables, the complete form of a kiss)

but-we-al-so-know-that-they-have-long-since-ac-quir-ed-the-ha-bit-of-co-la-bo-ra-ting-on-ly-with-much-re-ti-cen-ce

(sigh)

and-we-know-more-o-ver-that-a-mong-tho-se-who-claim-to-be-wri-ters-there-are-too-ma-ny-who-al-low-Me-mo-ry-to-con-duct-her-self-as-an-a-bu-si-ve-mo-ther

(another sigh)

as-soon-as-she-has-es-tab-lish-ed-her-self-in-their-works-she-reigns-as-mis-tress-and-for-bids-her-daugh-ters-to-ap-pear

(another, longer pause; the speaker's eyes sweep over the hall, looking for new marks of approbation)

it-is-in-or-der-to-at-tempt-to-find-a-new-so-lu-tion-to-this-pain-ful-fam-i-ly-con-flict-that-we-have-met-here

(third pause, immediately interrupted by bursts of laughter mixed with applause).

The audience, half of which consisted of young American teachers (and also a few who were not so young) on sabbatical, didn't need to hear any more to know that they were dealing with a Master.

Then, Flauzac laid his cards on the table. He set forth the main lines of his project: nothing less than the preparation and publication, within a period of five years, of a gigantic 'Analytical and Critical Dictionary of the Great Works in the Literatures (he regarded this plural as very important, for he included in it oral literatures, which he prized very highly) Of All Times and All Countries.'

Convinced that the insubstantial productions of his contemporaries would soon no longer satisfy people's appetites, he thought it was high time to reveal to the common reader the treasures of Arabic, Turkish, Egyptian, Japanese, Chinese, Albanian, Tibetan, Malay, and other literatures. And in his dreams of a permanent cultural revolution, he very clearly saw Chikamatsu dethroning Shakespeare and Ibn Khaldhun superseding Montesquieu, Jippensha Ikku competing with Rabelais and Wang Tch'ong with Hobbes, Isaiah and Ezekiel destroying Cicero and Demosthenes, and the pale attractions of European poetry (all countries lumped together) fading still further (if that is possible) before the matchless brilliance of the *qacidas* and the *rubayat*, of the *che* and the *ts'eu*, of the *waka* and the *zadjal*, not to mention the marvels of *haiku* and the *pantun*.

The work about which he had been thinking for years could be realized, he explained to the participants in the conference (whom goose pâté and Cahors wine, generously handed out by the prefecture's cultural office, had made very receptive to fraternal ideals and long-term enterprises), only through a series of stages whose rigorous succession he had determined as follows:

– *first: the drawing up, in each country taking part in the conference, and under the direction of a group devoted exclusively to this task, of an inventory of the texts worthy of mention;*
– *second: in each of the countries involved, an initial edition of the texts selected, to be printed in the form of a notebook with wide margins in order to allow later revisions;*
– *third: the circulation of these notebooks among all interested*

scholars and connoisseurs, whose comments were to be carefully collected and preserved;

— *fourth: the retention, in the final version, of everything that had not been challenged in any way; disputed points were to be discussed in a plenary meeting until a consensus view regarding them emerged;*

— *fifth: the reproduction, in the form of notes,* of the dissenting opinions, reflections, and complementary remarks.*

Thus we shall be assured, Flauzac concluded with grandiloquence (a grandiloquence that contrasted oddly with the jerky delivery of his exordium), *that nothing will ever tarnish the reputation of this monument, since it would reflect, with exemplary scrupulousness, the diversity of tastes and opinions of the world's most learned specialists,*

... you

(and as he pronounced it, this word suddenly seemed to have several syllables).

This finale delighted the audience.

The conference endorsed the project with enthusiasm.

The enthusiasm grew when it was announced how handsomely contributors to the project were to be remunerated.

Several hundred collaborators were quickly recruited. The enterprise thus began in an atmosphere of euphoria. But after two years, for reasons that remained mysterious (the blame was put on some people's incompetence, and on the extravagant demands of others), things began to go downhill. Of course, no colleague or financial group agreed to come to the rescue of *L'Herbe Tendre*, which, during the winter of 19——, withered and then died.

A few weeks later a couple of interesting bits of information

*It was later stipulated that to make them easy to consult, these notes would be placed at the bottom of the page.

emerged: *primo*, the woman who had been Flauzac's secret advisor since the beginning (she was even seen as having been the real inspiration behind the project), had left him; *secundo*, his former right-hand man, Valbert, who was only waiting for this failure, which had long been foreseeable (and he himself had done nothing, moreover, to delay it), had hastened to recuperate for himself, but with infinitely lower scholarly standards (and much less generous remuneration for contributors), the profitable part of the project.

Bruised, feeling lost in this milieu in which a man's stature seemed to be measured by his treacheries, and which in addition had never really pardoned his intrusion, Flauzac decided that he would have to leave Paris. Several provincial publishing houses tried to attract him: he was offered posts as literary director in Marseilles, Aubenas, Bourg-en-Bresse. Even the Crow, who had made up his mind to help him, submitted to him a long-cherished project: a vast encyclopedia (here he was staying on familiar terrain) that would systematically inventory all the plays on words that were possible in French. If it were just carried out with the required rigor and exhaustiveness, this kind of work seemed sure to be a commercial success, since almost all literary people would make it their bible. Flauzac didn't want to hear anything about it. He preferred to bury himself in his native Berry, where he spent several months in almost complete solitude.

I indicated to Sigmund that he could stop there. I knew the rest of the story.

Then the Crow, who had emitted several amused yelps while Sigmund was talking (especially when, transforming himself into Flauzac, Sigmund reproduced, caricaturing them, my friend's words and gestures, which I had never seen in such a glaring light), said in a sententious tone: *Yes, but all the same,*

*without Sophie, I don't know whether . . . Ultimately, it was she . . .
Well, that's what people said . . . Moreover, they said a lot of other
things about her, too, that were not necessarily true . . .*

I jumped. It quickly appeared to me, through several small
additional details that were incidentally mentioned, that he was
talking about the same Sophie: *mine*, if I may put it that way.
Now, I'd never, up to that point, had any reason to suspect that
she had any relationship with Gustave; neither of them had ever
said anything that suggested they even knew each other! What
a strange coincidence it was, I thought, that they had remained
silent regarding such an old relationship, and one that seemed to
have played, during the worst moment in Flauzac's life, a deter-
mining role. I tried to understand . . .

My friends had sensed my sudden discomfort, the reason
for which they did not know (few people knew how important Sophie was in my life). I did not dare tell them anything.
What good would that do? They understood that they'd better
leave. Which they did, almost immediately, leaving me with
my questions.

What kind of relationship had Sophie had with Flauzac? What
role had she played in his bankruptcy? And these rumors about
her, which were apparently hardly favorable, and which I was
hearing for the first time – what could they be? I was missing
something, for sure. An enigma that I suspected was important,
but which nothing yet allowed me to resolve.

I went back to my desk.

I found there, left among two empty cups, and its cover stained
with tea, what I now had to call, without a smile, *Book*. Finally
acquiring some embryonic information – the first, or almost the
first – about this curious work should have satisfied me, at least
for a moment. But it didn't. I was furious.

Book! The choice of such a title was just like all the rest! The same defiance, the same puerile effort to provoke. The vertiginous disproportion between this utterance of minuscule dimensions (nothing more, after all, than a four-letter word among others) and its literally infinite implications were enough to discredit the whole enterprise.

However, I gradually calmed down. I suddenly understood (I was becoming a seasoned reader) that it might well be a supplementary maneuver, a new ruse intended to drive me away, to make me finally give up.

Despite that, I was not sure (not at all sure, in fact) that it was fair to apply to books the strategy adopted by the builders of fortresses: by multiplying protections and defenses, one takes a risk as well: that of devaluing them, making them inoperative. To be sure, it's a noble ambition to try to surround yourself with mystery; but you still have to know how far to go, too much in such matters being worth hardly more than not enough.

After all, I said to myself, a writer may have the right to explore every path (usually a good pretext for exorcising at small cost one's liking for playing the fool, and also a good opportunity to allow one's touch of madness to ebb gently away), even to go astray, and in some cases to go down dead-end streets, but that doesn't mean that a sensible reader has any obligation to follow him in these divagations.

But this consideration was not enough to make me put the book aside. On the contrary: a force that I could not control was still acting on me.

FOURTH MOVEMENT

What one conceives well is not without sighs,
And the words to say it may well agonize.
— Boitaine

Some disguised falsehoods represent the truth
so well that it would be an error in judgment
not to let oneself be deceived by them.
— La Rochefoucauld

11

By now, I was tired of jumping around from one page to another, and in my hands, this little book was threatening to become as heavy as those marble books that appear, always open to the same page, on top of tombstones.

So I was ready to move forward.

The state of dissatisfaction in which the author had thus far taken pleasure in keeping me had effectively conditioned me: each new obstacle had succeeded, in fact, only in increasing my desire to overcome it. The time of questioning and irritation was giving way to that of impatience. I had crossed the Rubicon, and it was no longer a matter of strolling about, and still less of laughing.

But this time I was not going to interrupt myself. No matter what happened. Even if I had to skim quickly over the passages that shocked me, or that might, in one way or another, impede once again the progress of my reading. In short, I was ready to accept without blinking any new evasion.

Therefore I tried to read the whole book at one sitting, determined to get out of it every bit of substance it contained. My throat tight, and my mouth dry (despite several cups of tea drunk more or less mechanically). But I clung to my new determination as if to a buoy.

This proved not entirely useless: the author, who did not hesitate to create multiple false entries, had a couple more tricks for me in his pocket, and I had to weather a whole series of attacks. In the content, in the style, in the tone, each new page (up to and including the seventh) seemed to have been conceived only as a phase in the battle, a stage in the combat, as if, exploring all the resources of paradox and ambiguity, the author had tried to inventory, before coming to the heart of the matter, all the possible ways of challenging, confusing, and then discouraging even the most determined of readers.

Fortunately, however, the Pandora's box was soon empty. Before long I discovered that my author's stamina, in this area as in many others, was somewhat limited: after the seventh attempt, he gave up. No doubt his reserves of perverse imagination were exhausted; unless, perhaps, he finally realized that prolonging his stratagem would lead to nothing except a disguised form of suicide.

Thus, for me, the trial was less painful than I had at first feared. I did not regret my hazardous voyage through these pages, though so much had been done to keep me from beginning it. I even found in it something of the slight dizziness I used to feel when, playing tightrope walker and jumping (with uncharacteristic boldness) from building to building, I passed through, one by one, the white roof terraces of my neighborhood, on which long lines, taut as wires, held up rows of clothing and freshly washed sheets.

Naturally, this was not one of those massive, generous, and inflated works of wisdom that condensed the whole reality of a society, all the knowledge of an epoch, which each generation can further enrich by its own contribution. But I found in it no excess, no aggression, no acrimony (except, perhaps, toward the end, where several passages devoted to the sadness of growing old and the bitterness of being misunderstood went a little too far, for my taste, in exploiting easy opportunities for mockery and sarcasm). In short, none of the excesses I'd expected.

My discoveries were of another kind.

At first, it seemed to me that this volume, as a book, was merely an aggregate, at most organized into vague numbered sections (not even real chapters), of more or less autonomous pages. Each, like a human face, presented its own peculiar physiognomy, whose features, initially indistinct, came to life and grew clearer and more definite as the words and sentences fell into place. Nonetheless, they had a common characteristic: they seemed to have been composed hurriedly, and sometimes with headlong speed. One could not fail to be struck by what seemed to be a systematic, and immoderate, use of ellipsis.

Having dreamed of long, dense passages borne along by a broad impetus that nothing could interrupt, I constantly encountered instead pages in shreds, and in every case their content never exceeded, at best, a few paragraphs, two or three sentences, and was even reduced, at regular intervals, like a refrain, to a single line of ellipsis points. The most concise literary forms, clearly preferred because of the abrupt abridgements they allowed, were by far the best represented. The maxims, obviously written in turmoil and under the influence of a sudden sense of urgency, had retained a certain obscurity and a very archaic flavor. The arguments amounted to no more than a few words that surged up – only the beginning was given, and the rest was assumed to flow from it. Moreover, nothing was really developed or explicitly followed through to completion.

Naturally, the author had not felt, at any time, the need to explain this parsimony, this persistent concision (or if he did, it was in terms so allusive that I was unable to perceive them). Was it due to a congenital inability to write at greater length? Should the blame be put, as in the case of other celebrated authors of short texts, on his mental state, and his psychic health be gauged by the length of his aphorisms? Not a very flattering hypothesis, to be sure, but one which his opening pages did not allow me to set aside entirely. True, his book was only too much like the lovely little streams of my childhood, to whose banks my family

139

used to travel in the old black Chevrolet; there we picnicked on Sunday mornings, before the weather became too hot, and we quickly saw, on observing the slender, spasmodic flow of their springs, that they were unlikely to eventually broaden their beds to the dimensions of vast estuaries and one day flow, with a nuptial swoon, into the ocean.

But there might be other, less disobliging reasons for his choice. Why not suppose that this was a deliberate decision, made after a long and difficult education? Mistrusting the facility of writing at great length (as I suspected, without the slightest proof, he had done in his earlier works), he might have preferred to limit himself, regarding brevity and concentration as certain antidotes to the risk of mediocrity.

But his decision might also have been dictated by mere chance, by one of those serendipitous discoveries to which we owe so much. Residing in Paris, he might have suddenly understood, as he was strolling through the almost empty rooms of a Left Bank art gallery (divided, as usual, between the desire to stop every few steps to imbue himself with what was moving before his eyes, and the need constantly to move on in order to multiply his discoveries), that there are books like painted landscapes: they don't need to be filled out in order to be striking; a few strokes, which might at first be taken for a sketch, are sometimes enough to represent what needs to be represented. In this way, a secret dream would have been born within him: to equal the exploits of those virtuosos who are able to concentrate, in a wisp of straw more brilliant than a comet, or in a single paving stone whose belly shines gently under a streetlight, oceans of art.

The other distinctive mark of these pages (and there was no need to read all the way to the end to see this) was their dispersed, disjointed, in sum, their heterogeneous character. I immediately arrived at a diagnosis: since the author had tried to say everything all at once (and in every possible way) about what most deeply concerned him, this could only be a juvenile work . . .

In fact, the farther I read, the more I had the impression that I had come upon a real catch-all. A receptacle in which the most diverse materials were jumbled together: fragments of poetry (not many, at most *two or three sonnets more than Oronte*, with a clear preference for the most outdated symbolist clichés), but especially prose: fictions and confessions, interior monologues and apostrophes, accounts of dreams and erudite commentaries, maxims and moral reflections, truisms and paradoxes. Obviously, he had attempted to juxtapose several levels of experience, several levels of thought. And then left it to the reader to construct the bridges. As if he expected, from this interwoven mass, from the tension between these strata, something to emerge that he had tried to ensnare, something that could not otherwise be forced to show itself.

A diversity of content, but also a diversity of tone, of register, and even of grammatical genders (the general tonality being certainly masculine, though certain passages could only refer to a woman). The author ran, apparently without concern, the risk of contrasts, and even the most flagrant discords. With words intended to move (frail defenses erected against the disdain of learned readers, they seemed to act immediately on me, with the efficacity that I had earlier found only in my old store of magical formulas) were mixed words that had been concocted in order to explode in the reader's face, not to mention the words (too rare, alas) that must have been intended to amuse him. It occurred to me that if all these fragments were really written by the same person, they demonstrated, at the very least, his mastery of an extremely broad range and an incontestable aptitude for traversing genres, styles, and linguistic levels: this scarcely confirmed my initial diagnosis concerning the author's age, but that would certainly not be the first error I had made regarding this book . . .

There was a time when this mixture would have annoyed me immensely. I was not very fond of this explosion of forms, this abolition of boundaries, that had allowed so many illusionists to penetrate, through the breaches thus opened, into the literary field, and there to sow disorder. What good would it do for me to grumble about this return to the confusion of the Tower of Babel?

However, over the years I had gradually changed my attitude on this point. Here again, the return of some old memories had played a pacifying role. Ever since I was a child, one of my favorite texts had always been the *Song of Songs*; my father used to chant it every week. I listened to him religiously, so that even now, unexpectedly, I sometimes find myself repeating one of those old refrains whose melody and words one never truly forgets, and bits of which I like to hum:

A garden locked,
Is my own, my bride,
A fountain locked,
A sealed-up spring . . .

I sought, but found him not;
I called, but he did not answer.

One day, I had discovered with surprise, when I read the whole *Song of Songs* through, that I was utterly unable to assign it to a genre. An adventure story? A play? A liturgical chant? A love poem? I saw all these in it, and many other things besides, to which I used to be insensitive and which now only added, for me, to the seductive pleasure of the whole.

Thus I was ready to agree with those who proclaimed, sometimes with clarion trumpet flourishes, the bankruptcy of all literary forms, and ready even to find a certain attraction in the mixture of genres, provided that it was harmonious. But here there remained a major hitch: contrary to my beloved *Song of Songs*, the fragments of this strange work did not really seem to form any more than a poorly arranged amalgam. It was all disparity, fragmentation, diversity, dispersion. And at every turn.

The 'pensées' (how else can I designate these utterances?) referred to no identifiable body of doctrine. They even seemed to belong to at least two distinct groups.

Some of them would have liked to be taken for the miraculously preserved relics of an ancient, buried wisdom, and imitated its features in obscure proclamations:

Death, the closure of memory
Strong: the child of Bohemia among the Samurai
Locate a trickle of water in the ocean of erudition
Death, feel my sting
Sole place of residence: absence
Famine is not feigned
The shadow of death, white.

The others were produced, for the most part (for the author, who was very fond of formulas, was prepared to accept approximations) by twisting some banal utterance:

Anyone who has read much may have retained much
Someone who reads on Friday will weep on Sunday
Whoever steals an egg doesn't live on bread alone
A few steps from here are the most beautiful songs
A man who believes a greater fool's flattery is a fool

Worse yet, everything that had to do with writing (for he also offered, the wretch, a few remarks on this theme!) seemed to be a mixture of contradictory theories, picked up without discernment in various postwar avant-garde journals and with nothing in common other than having been long since rejected (except perhaps in literary circles in Aubenas).

As for the 'narratives,' they had hardly begun than they abruptly ended. The anticipated peripeteias, sometimes reduced to a single line, remained without consequence or justification:

When Narcissus was looking for his reflection in the eyes of passersby
Unable to sleep, spent his nights dreaming of the time when he slept
Swallow's nest seller, producer of counterfeits
Eager to take part in the race, camps on the starting line.

Finally, even the 'personal notes,' disregarding both chronology and logic, did not succeed in constituting the sketch of a diary or confession.

However, two short series of pages were exceptions to this rule. Inserted as if intentionally at the center of the work, they were the only ones in which a concern for homogeneity manifested itself.

The first series was a set of questions introduced by the same insistent formula: *Is it mere chance if?* A few of these questions seemed to me sufficiently unexpected and striking to be retained by my memory:

Is it mere chance if, in order finally to awaken, one has to have traversed the whole space of the dream?
Is it mere chance if the devil has everything it takes to make a world?
Is it mere chance if dreaming is the core of the irreversible?

The second set of questions appeared a few pages further on: a long series of assertions whose structure also consisted in the repetition of a single model, scarcely less simple (it combined three elements) than the preceding one. The author seemed to have found a convenient device for composing, through successive strokes and by emphasizing the features that distinguished him, a sort of fragmented portrait. I could not help being struck by some of these notations:

- *Perhaps you are one of those who are proud of being completely transparent. I'm not. Where would we find the truth of a being, if not in its opacity?*
- *Perhaps you are one of those who love heights. I'm not. Summits bore me, and I am dazzled only by a mass of fallen rocks.*
- *Perhaps you are one of those who attempt to narrate their childhoods. I'm not. My childhood narrates me.*
- *Perhaps you are one of those who hasten to arrive at their goal. I'm not. I like opportunities to learn what wandering never fails to teach: the schoolboy's way home doesn't seem to me so badly named.*

There were, it seemed to me, two or three dozen similar series, and they ought, more reliably than a classic assortment of piquant or edifying anecdotes, to provide a few keys to the author's personality, and at the same time, no doubt, the elements of a hidden autobiography. As if this peculiar author had wanted to show that he was foregoing (and with what disdain!) the opportunity to relive in toto, transmuted and magnified by writing, his life.

Thus I found in the book no more than traces. The traces of an itinerary whose stages seemed difficult to reconstitute, even in the most approximate way.

It was hard, under such conditions, not to wonder about the origin of these fragments, their status, and the reasons for which they had been assembled.

One day, when he was involved in a major straightening-up

(it might have been the day before, or after, a move), in the middle of a pile of cardboard boxes that had been neglected for a long time, he discovered, with considerable emotion, a few dozen old pages: thoughts written down in the euphoria that follows heavy drinking (the euphoria that makes us find a worn-out paradox fascinating, and the worst of puns full of meaning), recollections of childhood that had suddenly emerged from his memory (they must have been particularly dear to him, for he came back to them, it seemed to me, every time he could, and sometimes when they were entirely irrelevant), romantic intrigues conceived during a bout of insomnia and hastily transcribed in the early dawn. A whole collection of odds and ends (some elements of which probably dated from adolescence) that would probably have remained unemployed had he not used them in an 'oeuvre.' And what did it matter, after all, if this 'oeuvre' were to remain, in this case, largely fictitious, and even, so to speak, a sort of trompe l'oeil, since it would function only as a setting.

Not being able to resign himself to simply cutting out branches he knew to be nearly dead, nor to exhaust himself trying to give them life, he had limited himself to juxtaposing them, or rather to scattering them, delivering in bulk, and without the slightest polishing, the scoria of his aborted projects, of his failed literary experiments. But perhaps the task, in itself not very inspiring, of collecting these remainders had finally fallen to some local admirer, a childhood friend, a colleague or a disciple, who would have tried in this way to show posthumously his gratitude to his underestimated compatriot. I don't know what to call this unloading: a disenchanted balance sheet or a pious salvage effort.

And what if these pages had already been published? True, I had never discerned anywhere the slightest indication that they might have, but I was beginning to be familiar enough with my author not to be taken in by his tricks: this cagey silence regarding his sources smelled very much like a ruse! So nothing prevented me from formulating a new hypothesis. Maybe these pages came from earlier works, which he had had published by some obscure publisher(s) who had soon disappeared and been forgotten? Then, thinking they would never see the light of day in unabridged form, he might have sought to save some bits and pieces of them, some crumbs, the ones that seemed to him least unworthy of a somewhat prolonged life. In short, a little personal anthology, a reassuring mirror (unlike most mirrors) of a time when he had confidence in himself. If that were the case, I would have liked to know what criteria had guided him in making his choice. For I had every reason to fear the partiality of a man who thus made himself, without any witnesses, the embalmer of his own past work, using with complete impunity the redoubtable double weapon of memory and forgetting! For an author (as I had often noted, at first even with a certain surprise) is not necessarily, regarding his own writings, the best of judges or the most reliable of guides. Thus everything, in his work, became suspect, questionable: did these passages represent his thought directly? Was it really the same thought that was supposed to be expressed throughout? How could I judge the pertinence of a fragment without knowing what role it had played in the work from which it had been drawn? Wasn't he, intentionally, multiplying voices and points of view? And even if people other than the author were responsible for this volume, the same questions, obviously, arose. Questions that left me paralyzed.

Nevertheless, this dispersion continued to fascinate me. How could I explain that?

A coincidence, pure and simple? That was unlikely. To be sure, I said to myself, one doesn't always write the books one wants to write, not even those one thinks one is writing; but to this point . . . I even wondered whether what I was reading was really literature, whether what had been written belonged, for the person who had written it, to the category of letters.

And then the furious desire to disconcert, erected into the single source of inspiration? It is true that a taste for provocation sometimes leads you far away from your natural inclination. But to such a mess? I couldn't believe it.

To the point that I was tempted, repeatedly, to cross the barrier (increasingly diaphanous, I have to say) that still separated me from the book, and to intervene directly in the text.

Everything urged me to do so.

An old habit, which I'd acquired from too assiduous (and indeed, almost exclusive) frequentation of a very special kind of literature (the small cohort of those whom I called, with neither disdain nor derision, *writers for the rhetoric class*) led me to postulate, in any text, clarity and unity. Confronted by these confused pages, I was inclined to react as philosophers usually do when confronted by the spectacle of nature: by trying to rearrange the elements, to analyze the principle of distribution, hoping to find, beyond these disparate elements, a more or less rigorous system, based on predictability, regularity, and symmetry, even if they were (as sometimes happens) cleverly feigned or openly factitious.

Therefore I wished, not to set this chaos in order (that would have required a hero of quite a different stamp), but to make the necessary changes. It was less a matter of perfecting or improving than of completing a work that had, inexplicably, been left at the planning stage. So it was not, in this case, Correggio's often-cited outburst (*I, too, am a painter!*) upon seeing Raphaël's *Santa Cecilia* that could serve me as a motto. For at least he (I refer to Correggio) acknowledged that Raphaël was a painter. That was certainly not how I saw my scribbler! In fact, I had instinctively understood that I could free myself from this book's grasp only by finishing it.

Thus I obeyed what might well be called a reflex: whatever page I read, at first I saw in it only a provisional version, always open to retouching, of a text that had not yet been written (and that I, of course, had to write . . . some day). I have always felt a secret sympathy for those intrepid artists who, like Pierre Ménard, rewriting *Don Quixote* from beginning to end, or Colonel Godechot, translating *Le Cimetière marin* into 'French verse' (no less!), did not hesitate to get directly involved; but in this glorious lineage, the one I admired most was surely the hero of one of Jean-Paul's short stories, who, since he could not, in his remote country retreat, buy all the new books discussed in the newspapers he read, simply set about writing them himself . . .

And while I was bravely collecting sheets of paper and empty notebooks in order to get to work (it was no longer a matter of copying, but actually writing), I began to wonder whether that was not the hidden goal of this muddle so complacently displayed: to tell me that I was wrong to seek elsewhere than in my own effort; to force me to take over, pen in hand; to dislodge me, in short, from my comfortable status as a reader whose only task was to consume.

I had no difficulty in finding in the text things that responded positively to this new approach. A curious anecdote attracted my attention. It consisted of less than four lines: 'Edmond About, annoyed by the awkwardness of Balzac's writing, undertook to rewrite in his own way one of the volumes of the *Comédie humaine*. He decided on *La Cousine Bette*. His attempt resulted in the unforgettable *Germaine*.' His meaning seemed to me clear. The author was declaring, in this way, that he was simply ready to abdicate in my favor. To transfer to me, without further ado, most of his functions. He didn't want to make me his dupe, but rather his collaborator. This was, moreover, suggested, in the course of one page, in almost explicit terms: *At this moment, reader, I believe in you more than in myself.* Thus – this passage left no doubt – it was now up to me to complete the book the author himself had been unable to finish (for reasons that I still had to discover, but which I was beginning to glimpse).

A difficult task, to be sure. I felt like a spectator in a theater suddenly called upon, right in the middle of the play, to go up on the stage, redo the set, give the actors new instructions, change the content of their speeches, and even transform the very structure of the play that he has, in all innocence, come to see.

But then, who knows whether I hadn't finally grasped the real reason that had led my author to surround himself with so many precautions? Yes, his way of proceeding was much more understandable now. In his initial warnings, there was no paradox or provocation, only, on the contrary, a proper appreciation of the role that he was going to make me play. Hence the necessity that I show, at least by my perseverance, that I was up to the task. Since he expected two kinds of readers for this book, the right one was, evidently, the one who was prepared to get personally involved.

It seemed to me that I had just taken a major step.

But performing my new task seemed likely to take a long time: so many bridges to construct, so many gaps to fill in! Who knew how big I would have to make the book in order to overcome its fragmentation, its dispersal?

This kind of job could not be begun just like that, without the slightest previous preparation. I absolutely had to get in condition. So I began by going back to my bathroom, where I took a long bath. I took the opportunity to change my clothes completely. Without being as finicky as Buffon, who put on a coat and cuffs before taking up his pen, I was quite sure that my thought would be much clearer in a clean, freshly ironed shirt.

After an hour, my attempt at rewriting, at first limited to a few carefully chosen lines (the ones that alluded to early childhood), seemed to be bearing its first fruits. The author was coming nearer. We were beginning, he and I, to walk at the same pace. Better yet, I was already at the point where I no longer knew where his text stopped and mine began.

I tried to reread what I had just written. I was able to do so only with difficulty. Exactly as if these words, because they had been formed by my hands, were incapable of attaining the minimum level of objective existence that would have made them legible for me. And once again I had to resort to reading them out loud in order to see my own words take on substance and become autonomous.

Soon afterward, however, my enthusiasm encountered insuperable obstacles. How was I to succeed, with these meager fragments, in reconstituting the unity of a true book? I might as well have gone in search, at the foot of Mount Sinai, of the fragments of the Tablets that Moses, in his wrath, had broken!

It was absurd to persist; I had to resign myself and quit while I still could. For here I was dealing neither with a puzzle whose pieces I had only to assemble in order to achieve my goal, nor with one of those ancient mosaics that a big September thunderstorm sometimes (a rare windfall) relieves of the crust-hardened mud that obscures them, but with an object that had a quite different kind of complexity: a genuine excavation site, in which were juxtaposed, in complete disorder, the various stages of an old story, and, at the same time, the various stages of an ongoing research project.

By thus making clear his intent not to conform to any convention, by gaily mixing masculine and feminine, by not even foregoing, from time to time, the possibility of contradicting himself, the author sought to show that he was not one of those who are looking for a fixed form in order to wrap themselves up in it, as if to keep warm. Why would he want to give, at all costs, the illusion that his work was a rational construction? None of these laborious plasterings-over, none of the artificially created continuities, with which other people like to cover themselves. Order is not an ingredient that can be imposed on things a posteriori. He expressed this, in his own way, on one of his highly aphoristic pages: *Often the result of order is a beautiful disaster.* On the contrary. Adopting the practices of earlier ages, of which certain Baroque models must have inspired him (or at least have served him as guarantees), the author seemed especially concerned to constantly shift his book's center of gravity. And I wondered if behind all that there was not, very simply (and rather naïvely), the desire to produce an image of chaos, to mime in words the disorder of the world.

This was immediately confirmed by other observations. For example, the almost complete absence of genuine heroes. As if he had also wanted to do without these intermediaries, who were nonetheless so convenient, he had introduced, even in the fragments that seemed clearly to belong to the realm of fiction, only a few interchangeable puppets: each one, like the person who had, from the outset, tried to play hide-and-seek with me, seemed to be only a stage, an aspect, of a single individual (who was absent) containing them all.

In this way he obtained a curious effect of harassment. A kind of harassment that I was clearly not the first to feel. An earlier reader, far less respectful of the integrity of the printed page than I was (ever since my mother bought me, when I was about five, my very first *reader* – whose immaculate appearance I tried to preserve as long as possible, to the point that I forbade anyone to touch it – the slightest trace of a pencil point on a book has seemed to me an unbearable defilement), had not hesitated to soil the volume, in various places (about the same ones I would have chosen, had I allowed myself such reprehensible excesses), furiously crossing out words and adding exclamation points that amounted to cries of indignation. Like me, this reader had been exasperated by constantly losing the thread, by not being able to perceive the goal, and had condensed this exasperation by scribbling, on the last page, a single, irreversible judgment: *Hopeless*.

It was time to see things as they really were. Like a receding star, the book seemed constantly to be trying to escape from view. No, decidedly, the material object constituted by this little volume could in no way be transformed into the kind of impalpable intellectual reality that a book normally becomes as, enraptured, we read through it.

That is why the author found it impossible to put it in everyone's hands! This wretched pile of pages would probably have been laid aside very quickly . . . And, at the same time, crumbled into dust, like mummies that, as soon as they come in contact with the atmosphere, disintegrate. What good are readers, in a case where there is, properly speaking, no book?

I was ready to stop there, satisfied, when a new suspicion overcame me. What if the constraint represented by the unity of composition, too conventional to please our rebellious author, had been set aside only to yield to another, subtler form of unity? By searching everywhere for external marks of coherence, I had perhaps been repeating the error I had made the previous day, when I engaged in vain struggles with the opening page of this same book? Here, too, the apparent arbitrariness might very well conceal a strict determinism, but of another kind.

I'd thought I'd noticed, during my excessively voracious reading, the presence (discreet, to be sure, but with a very insistent, almost ostentatious, discretion, at times, despite the humble parentheses within which it pretended to sequester itself) certain themes (like everyone else, the author had trotted out, here and there, remarks on order and chaos, the meaning and lack of meaning of things), certain motifs (in one place, it was a secret that he was attempting to guess, in another, he sought an object that had been stolen, and in still another he unexpectedly found evidence of an event that had long been covered up), even a few parables (veils lifted or torn, rags, gowns, or hats riddled with holes) whose occurrence, although at first it seemed to me to follow no rule, was perhaps not due solely to chance. In this case, the variety of approaches, the rapid succession of fragments, always brief, would be easily justified: their function (a very delicate one) would be to render the fundamental unity of a 'message' less cumbersome, more digestible. Isn't the true reader one who is capable of constructing the place where dispersion takes on meaning?

Clearly, it was this hypothesis that I now had to test. An annoying task, which forced me to back up a long way.

I was aware, of course, that in doing so I was once again falling into one of the traps about which I had been warned at the outset. For I was now better able to gauge the fear the author might have felt in writing his exordium, and I imagined the cunning strategy this anxiety had forced upon him. Taking literally an old adage that he himself cited at least twice (*The only books worthy of the name are those that can be reread*), he had sought to produce a literary object such that its reader, disoriented by the first reading, could only immediately begin a second (and – why not? – many more afterward). In order to achieve this end, he would have liked, surely, to put in my hands one of those texts, as spare as they are fervent, whose success cannot be measured by the dose of illusion they can administer to the impatient visitor, and which, on the contrary, reveal their power only with sober deliberation. But not being able to risk counting on his talent alone (such an attitude would have required on his part an assurance he had not yet achieved, or, had he achieved it, would not have dared admit), he had preferred to use, as humble people often do in order to arrive at their presumptuous ends, artifices.

The chief of his artifices (I was now much better able to identify it) was the constant doubt he had succeeded in sowing in my mind regarding the nature of what I was reading: forced to wander amid these textual tatters separated by impressive quantities of blank space, I was confronted by a void that persistently refused to be filled.

The author knew what he was doing, then: He had wanted his book to be reduced to a simple shimmering, so that its existence was merely indeterminate, intermittent, and largely hypothetical. As if what counted for him was located elsewhere: in the possibility that he had thus created of moving forward, and of forcing me to move forward with him, as far as an extreme point beyond which any sort of rupture would be, for him and for me, impossible.

And in fact, this laborious trajectory, with its trials and its dead ends, its hopes, its successes, and its doubts, henceforth forbade me to lose interest in my adversary's fate.

12

Quid prodest brevitas si liber est. – Martial

It was to my author-adversary that I now wanted to turn. In order to illuminate, as in those good old works of literary criticism that I devoured as a teenager (and that are now very hard to find, even in used bookshops, which have also capitulated to current tastes), the enigma of the work by solving the enigma of the man.

Without having talked about himself in any way, he could claim to have handed out information, scattered allusions here and there: He exploited every pretext, every subject. But from each element he had deigned thus to provide, he had managed to make, in an almost mechanically regular reversal, the beginning of a question, having apparently understood that if he agreed, even for an instant, to set aside the ruses behind which his taste for anonymity was sheltered, he would find himself, at that very moment, in the uncomfortable situation of Noah taking off his own garment.

Despite all that, was I willing, for the sole pleasure (very selfish, I admit) of satisfying my curiosity, to start following him on a long quest? Usually, I'm not very fond of these belated investigations undertaken, in the name of Truth, by people intending to put things right, with no mandate other than the one they confer on themselves, and with the goal of revealing the hidden pettiness of great men and making fun of it. Have you done anything useful when you've succeeded, supported by all sorts of proof, in depriving someone of the aura of glory or mystery in which he has managed, throughout his life, to wrap himself, when you've reduced his image to the most deplorable banality? I don't think so. But in this case, I couldn't consider myself guilty of indiscretion or malice: I was not attacking a statue, as so many others do, in order to topple it; on the contrary, I was trying to do justice to an unfortunate author who had remained unknown.

For him – who had wanted to be without an identity, without a past, without any attachment, even more deprived of depth than the heroes of news items who are almost completely described once their identity, age, and profession has been given – I henceforth took pleasure in forging, using the materials I had found, an image. With the certainty that, even if juxtaposing poorly fitted elements did not suffice to produce a lifelike portrait of my author, he would not resent my efforts. I alone would bear the responsibility for the edifice I had erected.

So I saw him quite clearly, half dreamer, half rhetorician, caught between the contradictory demands (which were, moreover, already evident in the first pages of his book) of pouring out his soul and keeping it secret. Having succeeded, very early on, in taking sufficient distance from ordinary life to dare, at least internally, to see himself as a *creator* (a word the mere mention of which, in connection with his own name, must have felt like praise), he had first donned the mantle of a poet. But not, of course, one of those poets who appear in postmodern journals, those mechanical collectors of rare words and unheard-of images, whom he abhorred. No. Neither a seer nor a delinquent (Aubenas, obviously, was not Charleville). But an old-fashioned poet. A bard. Who would, had he not felt a certain residual fear of ridicule, have even carried a lyre in his hand and let his hair fall down to his shoulders, surrounded by a nimbus . . .

But the fairies had not hovered over his cradle. No tutelary goddess had benevolently provided him, at the right moment, with the weapons he needed for this kind of combat. Something inside him had refused to awaken, and time soon ceased to be gentle with him. Then, as he had not taken the trouble to put down any roots, one day he had found himself, without knowing quite how, and at the moment when he least expected it (which did not even allow him the meager consolation of saying that he had reached maturity without having sunk into any compromises), a pot-bellied forty-year-old. Having descended (somewhat abruptly) from his clouds, and more inclined to nostalgia than to hope, he at first gave himself up to a discreet melancholy (*If you think it's fun to be me! Let me tell you, it's hard, it's hard!*), hoping to make of his suffering a virtue and of his victim's mask a shield. Then, not really knowing whether he should henceforth use words as a means of evasion (as he had done up to that point) or as a means of vengeance (but on whom would he take vengeance, and for what?), he had found only one way out: to write only things that caused pain, to throw a harsh light on what he most desired to conceal (*I give in shamefully to my fears, and I do so in order to save myself*). As if he wanted incarnate, all at the same time, the handful of emblematic figures that pursued him: that of a gambler who wagers his last chip, the swimmer who touches the bottom, the shipwrecked man who clings to the last spar of his shattered vessel. Probably without suspecting that, by building on his defects instead of doing everything he could to overcome them, he risked going under, transforming into an inexpiable error what had been only a phlegmatic young man's mistake.

But he also had (for as we have seen, he was not afraid to contradict himself) the foible of those who have too much faith in the virtues of self-effacement and have long forced themselves to keep silent: for such people, each word ends up taking on a singular, excessive, disturbing weight; and if by chance they deign to indulge in language (*Writing: too serious a matter to be*

159

left to writers), they have a lamentable tendency to take themselves for oracles. And so he was driven by the illusion that leads some people to think they are the bearers of new truths. A kind of people I normally distrust, without, however, being able to prevent myself from listening to their sermons.

I had been struck by certain sentences that, despite the appearance of objectivity in which they were enveloped (*I still fear I may have written only a sigh when I think I have noted down a truth*), had, for the trained ear (and mine was becoming better trained with each page), a confident tone: *All oeuvres are posthumous, and nothing one agrees to reveal is ever more than advance notice.*

Thus he had written without being the apostle of any cause, trying simply to think constantly against himself, and if need be, against thought itself (a path that perhaps went back to some very old memories), reserving for his rare whiffs of inspiration, when they managed to overcome the censorship he imposed on them, the bulk of his sarcasm. Not being able to build, stone by stone, some vast and grandiose edifice in which countless motifs would be intertwined (they would be so laced within one another that one could not separate them without imperiling the very fabric of the book), in which would be fully apparent the acuteness of his vision, his ability to resituate, in their truth, the most diverse aspects of life, he turned round and round in the miniscule prison he had constructed himself, a prison whose exiguity he could not forget because he had, on all its walls, installed fragments of mirrors.

I wondered why he had not been better received by his peers, why he had not become more closely connected with the horizon of his time (which is also ours, after all), which was, nonetheless, so open to this kind of thing, why his crossing of the desert seemed to have been even longer than his life: What crippling absence of agreement between what he had to say and his potential audience had created this chasm?

One thing seemed clear: his vocation, insofar as it could be discerned, was not to add to the number of those who make their entrance, establish themselves, and prosper. Around him, many people must have found, and rightly, some of his commitments irritating: the asceticism that led him to pretend to suspend any search for meaning (*Where is it hidden, then? no response other than a feeble echo of my questions*) and to take an interest solely in problems of form; the claim that he was addressing, over the heads of all his contemporaries, generations to come, assumed to be capable (by what mysterious privilege?) of greater discernment; and, above all, the concern, pushed to the point of obsession, with imposing on the unfortunate reader, by all available means, including the least common and even the least fair (for instance, the constant braking of the discourse, with his series of sentences which, their every tiny particle being stuffed full of suggestions, seemed to have embarked upon the elucidation of some serious problem, whereas in reality, eluding it, they only amplified, gradually, through a series of echoes, cleverly arranged and coordinated like so many imperceptible intermediaries, the void), the duty to search for something in the book other than its apparent absence of content. Thus ballasted, he had not been able to surmount the barricade erected by the critics or by his audience. And so he had remained marginal: on the threshold of some other place that was always near, but never attained.

There vaguely emerged, a reversed, intaglio image of a man who had taken as his sole task (and this seemed to be, for him, a constantly repeated effort, a constantly renewed activity) to disappoint. Could I really blame him, or cast a stone?

I had thought I was on the right track when I imagined that he had constructed his work as others construct a dirty trick; I saw clearly that, instead, I had to divine, behind all the illusionist's trappings, an old charlatan with lifeless eyes, sincerely believing that he was waging a war against himself that could not be won.

What he seemed not to have foreseen was that ultimately, he would be found out. For I was well aware, now, that he was going to continue to indulge in his favorite exercise. A mountebank's trick, long since given away! So obvious, in fact, that I wondered again whether there wasn't something fishy here.

And then, suddenly, something new (once again) dawned on me. From the beginning, I had been floundering about in complete illusion. Everything I had just constructed (and with what difficulty!), by shamelessly adopting the worst clichés of old-fashioned criticism (the kind that is still sometimes stigmatized with the barbarous adjective *psychologizing*), was nought but wind and the pursuit of wind.

In accordance with my old habit, I had missed the essential point.

I had, in fact, picked out, from the pages I had used to reconstitute this not very splendid portrait, a whole series of sentences that sounded more than familiar to my ear. And with good reason! They seemed to have been drawn from my most private notebooks, the ones to which, up to that point, only Sophie (and even then on very rare occasions) had had access.

I rubbed my eyes. Wasn't I about to succumb to the illusion to which, since my childhood, I had often fallen victim, and which made me take for memories surging up from a more or less distant past, events I was actually currently experiencing? In the past, it had played more than one trick on me, but recently it had seemed to be leaving me alone.

No, there was no possible doubt. I knew these sentences. I

162

even remembered, for some of them anyway (*Vision is the art of seeing the invisible, the true language is the one that leads us to understand something other than what it says*), the works in which I myself had found them, the moment when I myself had felt the need to copy them out. To be certain, all I had to do was open one of my thick notebooks bound in black cloth. Thus I was suddenly sent back, at the moment when I least expected it, to my most personal ruminations.

This revelation revolted me: I felt robbed. Yes, evicted from whole parts of my past, of my thought. Secret parts, which someone, who seemed to know me from the inside, had laid hands on without my knowledge, and that he had stitched together any old way, amid a jumble that had no connection with me.

What to do?

I would have liked to be able to pull out, to scream. No, to be sure, I had nothing to do with these pages, I was only a chance passerby, a rubberneck, whose curiosity made him hang around the scene of a show not meant for his eyes . . . But no sound came out of my mouth. And I continued to read, more and more attentively.

This time, the sentences that seemed disturbingly familiar increased in number. I was sure I had already read them else-where, in just the same, or slightly different, form. I was even ready to attach a name to some of them: Stendhal here, Sachs and Michaux later on, without mentioning Blanchot, Montaigne, Char, Schopenhauer, and a few others.

So who knows if the whole book (with perhaps the exception of the opening pages on which I had so long labored) had not been produced by an analogous method? Rather than an account of things thought or experienced, an inventory of sentences read? A more or less faithful collection of the texts in which my anonymous author had once recognized himself? He, too, must have savored the acute pleasure I had discovered as a teenager (but which grips me far more frequently today) when, all at once, some circumstance of my life seems to have been expressly intended to illustrate and confirm, with incredible appropriateness, some remark that had struck me in reading the work of a beloved predecessor.

Now the more I pored over these pages, the more my impression was confirmed. They seemed to me to have come straight out of a regular anthology, or rather one of the reading notebooks that conscientious tutors used to put together: a treasure patiently accumulated that can be drawn upon in accord with the needs of the moment. It was hardly surprising if I found in it neither the unity I was looking for nor the personality I was trying to determine.

So that's why the fellow from Aubenas, tormenting himself again, had taken refuge in anonymity! From a residual sense of modesty, probably, he had not dared to put his name on this book composed of borrowings: it was indeed the least he could do, in his situation. But why didn't he use, I wondered, a borrowed name? He had apparently hesitated to adopt that sordid expedient, and that made me find him more likeable.

Urged to publish, he had not taken the time to write, or even thought it necessary to try to write. He had preferred to compile. Unscrupulously embracing the spirit and the method that brought glory to the postman Cheval, he had done no more than assemble the scattered materials he had collected in the course of his daily rounds in the world of letters, limiting himself to a few insignificant modifications.

His procedure, reconstituted in this way, left me pensive. It was unusual, of course, but, was not without very honorable models, when you thought about it. It only continued, shifting it

164

to a higher level in the scale of literary objects, the attempt made by certain poets who, having decided to let language do their thinking for them, built their oeuvre on the basis on groups of words thrown like handfuls of confetti onto the all-too-blank paper. The result was the kind of simulacrum I held in my hands: its lack of literary substance could no longer in any way detract from its incontestable material presence.

I finally understood Flauzac's interest in this book, and why he had sent it to me: my pitiful author had in fact never ceased to be a reader. But a very special kind of reader. Curious, passionate, bulimic.

I was now burning with a new desire: to see if the author's harvest was a match for his readings. Therefore I had to resume my exploration immediately, throw myself into the search for the origin of each of these fragments, and restore them to their true author (perhaps that was the real secret of the book)!

A desire that was increased by the feeling that I had to take up a new challenge, one that was, this time, entirely within my reach.

13

When what you are reading elevates your mind,
and inspires noble and courageous feelings, don't look any
further for a rule by which to judge the work: it is good,
and made by a master hand.
– La Bruyère

I was starting to move backwards when I heard my door open. It was written, clearly, that this day would not be an ordinary day! Smiling, more beautiful than ever, a bunch of white roses in her hand, Sophie came into my apartment.

I had long since given up hope of seeing her.

She couldn't have come at a worse time. Throughout the preceding day and most of the night, I had waited (with what impatient fervor!) for her to come. And now, without any warning, here she was, flowers in her hand, at the precise moment (perhaps the first since our love affair had begun!) when I would have liked to have a few more moments of solitude.

For I felt that the confrontation with my adversary – an adversary all the tougher because he was elusive – was nearing its end. I was on the right track. All I needed was a couple of minutes. Just long enough to enter, armed with my explorer's staff, the heart of this book. To search its most secret recesses. In order to make it show what it was made of. And finally, to set my mind at ease about it . . .

Now that Sophie was there, I was going to be obliged to leave everything at the planning stage, and put off this adventure until God knew when. And the delights of the solution that I had been tenaciously trying, since the preceding day, to discover, would be delayed by just that much. So, farewell to the much-anticipated reward of my meritorious efforts!

But I can't help it – I can't bear unfairness. And above all, I don't like to be deprived of the pleasure of carrying my projects through to the end. There's nothing more intolerable than the shock of interruption, than the bitterness of having to postpone pursuing a relationship just when it has begun to go well. I'd been forced to endure this kind of suffering so often, mainly while traveling, that it had become odious to me. And as Sophie came nearer, some memories with a melancholy taste surged up (most inopportunely, I admit). One, in particular, that had imbued with bitterness the final hours of my stay in Sirolo two years before.

As was my habit, I had gone off, in the early morning, to an isolated rock, far from the shrieks of the children playing ball, far from the eyes of the families huddled under the endless rows of umbrellas, to read a story by Calvino that was set on precisely this beach. At the hottest time of the afternoon (the time when, in an instant, the beach chairs empty and the wooden benches in the trattorias fill up), there came to sit near me, to my great surprise (since on the preceding days, other people on the beach had scrupulously respected my clear desire to be left alone), a young woman, with naked breasts and red lipstick, whom I pretended not to notice. But almost immediately, putting down the magazine she had, as if for appearance's sake, quickly glanced through, she began, on various pretexts, and with persistence, to speak to me. At any other time, this kind of thing would have delighted me, and I would have welcomed my charming intruder with the warmth that I reserve for women who are able to approach me spontaneously. But at that moment, I was only a few pages (three or four) from the end of my story, and an unexpected reversal (I, at least, had never expected it) had just occurred. I wasn't interested in anything but finishing the story: I was so impatient to discover – in order to assess it, as a connoisseur – how the author was going to land on his feet! Despite the annoyance evident in my initial replies, whose laconic nature left no doubt as to my attitude (a shrug of my shoulders, two grunts and three monosyllables), Francesca (I was soon to learn that this was her name) finally overcame my virtuous resistance. I said a few words. We quickly discovered that we had seen each other two days earlier at the home of some mutual friends, who came, as she did, from Rimini. Then things between us took, with a rapidity that astonished me (exactly as if some clandestine orchestra director had suddenly decided to accelerate the tempo of the music we were to play on that day), such an intimate and passionate turn that I never did find out what happened in the rest of my story. For while my attention was thus entirely focused on my enterprising companion, who quickly managed to obtain from me some of the attentions she wanted (and which she seemed – inexplicably, in my view – not to have received since she had arrived in Sirolo), the sea, discreetly but ironically sneaking up on me, had carried off my abandoned book, dropping it a few moments later amid the pedal-boats, rubber kayaks, and windsurfing boards. And, at the end of the afternoon, after giving Francesca a last kiss, I had to leave the beach alone, satisfied but disappointed.

The same disappointment, which I was not able entirely to conceal, must have been visible on my face. Sophie perceived it immediately. As soon as I went up to her and leaned down to kiss her, she stiffened, and looked at me intently, with a slight, inquisitive frown. I immediately lowered my eyes. Not a word had been uttered. For the first time since we had met, Sophie found me not happy to see her, and wanted to know why. I didn't feel able to tell her all that had happened to me over the past two days: that would have given her an image of me that was anything but heroic.

She lingered in the room for only a few minutes, walking around as if looking for something. Then with her usual celerity, she moved toward the door, which had been left open, and departed. Still without a word.

I tried to run after her. I stumbled over a volume of my old *Larousse* encyclopedia (volume 8, F–GYZ, one of the thickest), which had been lying on the floor for the last three days (I had been trying, in vain, to find information on Fuzuli). When I managed to get up again, despite the pain in my ankle, the elevator door had just closed on Sophie. I hobbled down the stairs. I was able to catch her only at the exit from the building. She was inflexible: she wouldn't listen to my explanations or accept my excuses, and finally jumped in a big black taxicab that seemed to be waiting for her alone.

This was the kind of incident I feared most. I was well aware that such things left indelible marks that all the sincerity in the world is unable, later on, at the crucial moment, that of the inevitable reconciliation, really to erase. But the harm was done, and I had to make up my mind what to do.

I knew Sophie: she would quickly draw from all this the conclusions that seemed to her inevitable and would not fail to communicate them to me immediately. So once again, all I could do was wait.

The cold had become sharper, and the streets were deserted. I don't know how long I wandered around the neighborhood, with which I was still not very familiar. I walked slowly, without seeing where I was going. I was trying to draw my own lesson from these events.

Since the beginning, that confounded book had brought me nothing but trouble. I should never have let such a calamity enter my home! It was time to have done with it. To destroy it. To rip it into tiny pieces. Page by page. Throw it all to the winds. And do everything I could so that no one could pick up the smallest scrap. Or else (why not?), burn it. Yes, I could make a nice bonfire with these absurd pages. My first auto-da-fe: a strange day, to be sure, in the life of a book lover! Where had I read this remark, whose meaning I finally understood: *To put the finishing touch on a book is to burn it?* The idea started running through my mind. Rapidly, it took complete possession of my thoughts. Fire! Fire, to get rid of this troublemaker. I'd made my decision. I hurried back to my apartment.

I was almost there when I saw, down a little one-way street I'd not yet had an opportunity to explore, a storefront that looked like a grocer's or a wineseller's. My supply of tea, after the visit of my two brilliant cryptographers, was exhausted, and I also had no alcohol. So I started down the street. But only to discover, very quickly, that the shop towards which I was heading was in fact a Quick Repair Shop that exhibited, in its dusty display window, a pile of kitchen utensils and household appliances from the period right after the war. While I was looking over this junk, trying to identify two or three objects I'd have sworn came out of a Carelman catalog, I was grazed by a car, its motor roaring. The driver, apparently as distracted as she was hurried, had started down the street the wrong way, and, abruptly backing up, had nearly run me over. She disappeared before I had time to tell her what I thought of her.

So I climbed the stairs to my apartment, empty-handed, and locked myself in.

The hour of the great settling of accounts had arrived: at last, I was going to be able to prove my determination. I wanted to snatch up my little book, I was ready to inflict on it with my own hand (which was already trembling, poor thing) the punishment it richly deserved.

171

Then I noticed that it was no longer where I thought I'd put it down when Sophie unexpectedly arrived.

I began to search for it, with growing concern, in the various recesses of my office.

Couldn't find it.

All the other books I'd had occasion to dip into over the preceding days were there: a large number of literary reviews from the 1940s, a few more recent issues of *L'Arc*, an old edition of Lessing's *Laocoön*, with a bookmark at page 36 (I admit that I had not been able, despite all my efforts, to compete with Goethe, who claimed to have read this essay three times in a row on a single day . . . For my part, I'd given up long before the end of the second reading). But no *Book*. It had disappeared. Purely and simply *dis-ap-pear-ed*.

I should have been happy about this. It spared me the melancholy act that a moment of fury had led me to plan. There was no longer any need, now, for an auto-da-fe . . .

I could also have seen it as unimportant: there was certainly no lack of books in my apartment, any number of which could advantageously replace that one . . .

But that wasn't how it was.

I was dumbfounded, and the silence of my apartment suddenly fell upon me with unaccustomed weight. At first, I felt cut to the quick, as if I'd been personally insulted by such a nimble spiriting-away. And then, this disappearance put everything back in question: it lent a new dimension to everything that had just happened.

Someone must have come into my place during my brief absence (although I hadn't noticed, when I returned, any sign of an effort to break in, and nothing in my office had been disturbed). Someone who knew that this obscure little book existed, and that it was in my apartment, had thought it necessary to make off with it, precisely on that day, at that moment. Why? Obviously, not because of its value. Well, then? Wasn't it because it had become absolutely necessary to get it, immediately, out of my sight? But what perils did it conceal, then, beneath its disguise as an old relic?

The trap announced in the first line of the book was really there, this time. And as planned, it was closing on me. In the most classical way possible. Every step I'd taken had helped fate realize itself, at the very moment I thought I was averting it.

At the same time, however, I could not resign myself to believing in that much depravity. On the contrary. The book's sudden aura of mystery sufficed to make it precious to me again. And as full of hope as it had been a few hours earlier, at the moment of intense emotion when I was getting ready, defying the initial prohibition, to move on to the second page. I would not now accept, for anything, seeing it close up again, disappear, taking with it its incompletely revealed secret.

And I was obliged to recognize that with all its provocations, anomalies, and inadequacies, of which there were more than enough, it had never left me indifferent. Better yet, it had managed to awaken in me so many forgotten memories, so many thoughts I didn't know I had within me, and which, but for it, would never have seen the light of day!

I was now ready to make amends.

No, it was not, as I had thought, one of those empty trompe-l'oeil constructions, composed to trap, through the somewhat perverse pleasures they offer, a few dazzled gawkers. Far from being closed in upon itself, it seemed to me, on the contrary, retrospectively, to be provided with a whole arsenal intended to increase my discernment, and even to make my eyes better able to resist the seductions to come. Something like gratitude was being born in me and sought a way to manifest itself. What strange power did it have, then, this book, to put me in such a state?

I had to find it. Right away. No matter what it took.

Oh, I knew well enough that there might be something ridiculous about this sudden ardor coming after fear. If Sophie knew! If she could see me at this moment! She would probably think I was drunk, and would try, assuming her calmest manner, her most persuasive voice, gently to bring me back to rationality. But, as was my habit, I would find plenty of models to justify my enthusiasm. You couldn't count all the people, even among my own friends, who had been the victims of this kind of singular passion. One, lost in the African desert, had fallen in love with a magnificent lioness, another had fallen in love with a simple figure of a young girl he'd seen on a Pompeian bas-relief, and still another had fallen in love with a newly exhumed Venus; at the Flauzacs' house, an old servant who had died while worshiping her stuffed parrot was even remembered. After all, since so many people have become infatuated with the heroes and heroines of novels, why shouldn't I have the right to be concerned about a book with which I had just spent several hours of my life? And also about its author, a man in whom I now saw less an enemy (oh, how I regretted having allowed myself, after that unfortunate beginning, to launch, on someone I had too hastily taken for a lout, a bitter attack!) than my double?

I began to imagine all sorts of explanations. Someone must surely have been trying to get me, someone who knew me well, since he had known how to find my weak spot and had taken the trouble to strew before my feet obstacles intended to make me stumble.

Questions immediately arose that made me feel dizzy. I saw the book as a sort of bomb, a fire ship. But whose effects, perversely, appeared only later on. One of my friends had once

174

conceived the idea of a detective novel in which the murderer would ultimately turn out to be the reader. I was afraid that I was dealing with an equally unprecedented case: the one in which the reader is . . . the victim.

Who knew whether this book had not been deliberately conceived, in its presentation, its content, and even its sudden and theatrical disappearance, to put me to the test, to assess my reactions? All that might well be only the unfolding of a small, carefully elaborated hoax. On the part of whom? Enemies? Friends? But what exactly were they trying to do? What did they expect from me, or from their deception? That it would cure me, turn me away from books? Apparently, no matter how well informed they were, they didn't know they'd come too late for that: I had already reached, quite a long time before, that stage in the illness when the remedy is what the patient finds most repulsive.

As my meditations concluded, I couldn't help returning to Flauzac. It was from him that I had to demand an explanation, and perhaps an accounting. For it was he, I was now almost sure, who must be at the origin of the whole business, which was beginning to look to me like a conspiracy.

This time, I had to call him. Immediately.

At Flauzac's place, the phone rang for a long, long, long time. When someone finally decided to answer it, I did not at first recognize Flauzac's voice. He must not have recognized mine, either, for he had me repeat my name three times. And right afterward, without giving me time to say anything, he drew me, in a melodramatic tone that I'd never heard him use, into the following dialogue:

Him: My poor friend! I was expecting you to call. You don't understand a thing about what's happening to you, right?

Me (hardly surprised by his perspicacity, and confirmed in the notion that it was he who was pulling the strings): Well, yes . . . I admit that I had begun to hesitate, to doubt, right from the beginning.

Him: Really? But it didn't start out so badly for you! Quite a siege, huh?

Me: Yes, but there were so many possibilities, so many avenues opened up . . .

Him: Things are clear, now.

Me: On the contrary! Now I don't know where I am. So I beg you to tell me everything. Admit it, and reassure me: it was you who set up this whole affair?

Him: Not at all! I wasn't involved in any way. My only role was to console you – afterward!

Me: Nonetheless, if possible, I'd like to try again, and start over from the beginning.

Him: No! That could only hurt you. Don't think about it. Don't give it another thought . . . I'd have liked to be able to help you. But, believe me, there's no other way to deal with these things, there's nothing you can do.

I felt he was nervous, eager to hang up. Then I tried a last question.

Me: But can you at least explain one thing to me, anyway?

Him: What?

Me: What's so extraordinary about this book?

Him: What are you talking about? What book?

Me: Well, the one I've been talking about all along, of course: one of those you gave me last summer and that has strangely just disappeared from my office. It was called, precisely, *Book*.

Him (at first, with a great deal of irritation in his voice): I never gave you a book with that ridiculous title . . . (then, the voice trying to sound normal): If you want my advice, I'd say you should take it easy for a while.

And he hung up.

I called him back immediately. This time he answered right away. Flauzac practically barked at me:

'Haven't you understood yet that Sophie has left for good? She came to tell you herself; but you weren't, apparently, ready to listen to her. She came back shortly afterward and didn't find you. So she wrote to you. And then she called me to ask me to look out for you . . . '

Flauzac was still talking when the doorbell rang.

It was, accompanying my key (slipped into a tiny blue envelope bearing my name in capital letters), a message from Sophie. Every word wounded me:

Why wait any longer? I'm leaving. Greece was not such a bad idea after all. But without you.

I'm depositing with you the only useful thing I can still offer you: my silence.

Farewell.

Sophie.

P.S. *I took back the little pamphlet I left on the corner of your desk last week.*

CODA

Please, leave me alone, you people who
manufacture, by the dozen, forbidden rebuses, whose
frivolous tricks I did not at first perceive, as I do today.
A pathological case of incredible egotism.
— Lautréamont

In the *Stages* series